Breaking Boundaries

Theological Inquiries

Studies in Contemporary
Biblical and Theological Problems

General Editor
Lawrence Boadt, C. S. P.

PAULIST PRESS
New York • Ramsey • Toronto

Breaking Boundaries

*Male/Female Friendship
in Early Christian Communities*

Rosemary Rader

PAULIST PRESS
New York • Ramsey • Toronto

Copyright © 1983 by Rosemary Rader

Library of Congress
Catalog Card Number: 82-60756

ISBN: 0-8091-2506-4

Published by Paulist Press
545 Island Road, Ramsey, N.J. 07446

Printed and bound in the
United States of America

Contents

Dedicated to my parents,

Cecilia Margaret Skrypek

and

Anton Joseph Rader

and to

Lawrence, Marie, Eugene,
Paul, Ruth, Sister Cecile Marie,
Frances and Don,
Herman and Millie,
Henry and Keiko,
Lawrence E. and Marley,
Alfred,
Joseph and Hilaria

in gratitude
for their
familial love and support

Preface

My interest in the present study began at Stanford University as I researched the dissertation topic, "The Role of Celibacy in the Origins and Development of Christian Heterosexual Friendship." After I completed the dissertation and began teaching courses in Early Christianity at Arizona State University, I realized that more issues were involved in the friendship phenomenon than I had fully realized, particularly issues dealing with changes which occur in ideals, attitudes, and customs as a new movement proceeds through its formative stages. As I taught about the social world of the early Christians I was forced to reevaluate much of the material dealing with changes in the status and roles of both women and men. This book is the result of ruminations, further research, and discussions on changes in male/female relationships in the world of the early Christians.

The study would not have been completed without the invaluable aid of William A. Clebsch who consistently challenged ideas and assumptions undergirding the study. To him I owe a special thanks. I also acknowledge my appreciation for the encouragement and insights of Peter Brown, Elaine Pagels, Elizabeth Clark, Amanda Porterfield, Lee Yearley, Mary Jane Bright, and a host of other generous colleagues, students, and friends.

The writing of the book was made possible by a summer grant in 1975 from the Institute for Ecumenical and Cultural Research in Collegeville, Minnesota, by a grant from the Mrs. Giles Whiting Foundation for research in Rome, Italy, during 1976–77, and by a Faculty Grant-in-Aid from Arizona State University for Summer 1979. I also want to thank the library staff members at Stanford, the Monastic Microfilm Library, the Vatican Library, and the American Academy in Rome.

1

Introduction

Much has been written within the last several decades about the experiences, contributions, roles, and status of women within the early Christian tradition. Most studies, however, have dealt almost exclusively with male/female dichotomy as evidenced in ecclesiastical forms of ministry and positions of authority.[1] To concentrate on literature which deals specifically with ecclesiastical organizations, hierarchical structure, administrative policies and Church institutionalization is simply to eliminate women from consideration. What seemed historically significant to the male authors of the period (i.e., power structures and spheres of influence in political and economic affairs) dealt with those aspects of Christian life where women had little or no impact. Although a teasing of such texts might present important insights about women, there are other primary sources which explicitly or implicitly offer more direct evidence of a feminist heritage within early Christian societies.

Until very recently history has been so defined as to include only those aspects of human experience in which men were active. Women's activities were deemed less necessary and therefore peripheral to the narration of history. That notion has been subjected to intense scrutiny as social historians began to redefine the standard of human history to include both male and female activities.[2] Con-

---

1. These studies generally attempt to evoke historical precedent as justification for either maintaining or changing the status quo on such issues as clerical celibacy or ordination of women. Cf. Joan Morris, *The Lady Was a Bishop* (New York: Macmillan, 1973); Elaine Pagels, *The Gnostic Gospels* (New York: Random House, 1979); Rosemary Radford Ruether and Eleanor McLaughlin, *Women of Spirit: Female Leadership in the Jewish and Christian Traditions* (New York: Simon and Schuster, 1979); Carroll Stuhlmueller, ed., *Woman and Priesthood: Future Directions* (Collegeville, Minnesota: Liturgical Press, 1978).

2. See particularly Sheila D. Collins, "A Feminist Reading of History: Sources of

vinced that there is nothing sacred about historical content which deals exclusively with male experiences, historians have begun to research and write about those aspects of the past in which women have been active participants. That is, historians have begun "to write about aspects of the past in which women have figured prominently and in their own right: the family, the working force, reform movements, religion, and education—in short, social history."[3]

One such area of social history is the phenomenon of male/female friendships within the Christian communities of the third through the fifth centuries. There is much literary evidence in subapostolic and patristic literature attesting to the existence of heterosexual friendship, a reciprocal relationship of affection between individuals which was not dependent upon, though not necessarily devoid of, sexual attraction. These recorded instances of close interpersonal relationships between men and women appear to have been founded upon mutuality of goals which minimized or eliminated the inequalities inherent in sexually differentiated societies, and thus allowed for friendship between men and women.

This was significant in that most cultures around the time of Christ fostered a climate inhospitable to authentic friendships between men and women. Social conditions were such that, except for some notable exceptions, men and women's interchange of ideas and amiabilities were confined to the home. The paradigm of male/female relationships was the exclusive husband/wife one. This orientation toward a single exclusive relationship diminished the significance and the possibility of extramarital and non-sexual friendships between men and women. The present study undertakes to analyze this phenomenon by establishing the particularities of its origins and developments as depicted in specific literary instances.

Values for a Different Revolution," *Radical Religion*, 1 (Spring 1974), 13–15, and *A Different Heaven and Earth* (Valley Forge, Pennsylvania: Judson, 1974); Bernice A. Carroll, ed., *Liberating Women's History: Theoretical and Critical Essays* (Chicago: University of Illinois Press, 1976); Carl N. Degler, *Is There a History of Women?* (Oxford: Clarendon, 1975); Valerie S. Goldstein, "The Human Situation: A Feminine Viewpoint," *Journal of Religion*, 40 (April 1960), 100–12; Rosemary Radford Ruether, *New Women/New Earth: Sexist Ideologies and Human Liberation* (New York: Seabury, 1975).

3. Degler, p. 6.

CHAPTER ONE

Heterosexual Friendship: Distinctive Phenomenon Within Early Christian Societies

True friendship, by definition, presumes a sense of equality. Whether it is the biblical example of David and Jonathan, or the classical Greek depiction of Achilles and Patroclus, the relationships demonstrate an attitude of reciprocal affection and respect. History abounds with instances of close, interpersonal relationships between specific individuals whose mutual affections are able to traverse the normative racial and social boundaries, with but one exception. The model friendships are those between men. The boundaries of male and female are rarely crossed, and in the rare instance when this does occur there is a suspension of the norms of male/female relationships. Several of the noted spokesmen of Western European cultures (e.g., Plato, Aristotle, Cicero, Augustine, Montaigne) reflect the prevailing notion that by nature friendships could not exist between persons of the oppostie sex.

Early Christian literature from the third to the end of the fifth century demonstrates notable exceptions to the rule.[1] There are numerous depictions of heterosexual friendship which give the particulars of its origins and developments. What is more difficult to discern

---

1. The third century has been chosen as the *terminus a quo* because literary data about friendship had by then become available; the fifth century serves as a convenient *terminus ad quem* because by that time the more liberal, egalitarian type of heterosexual relationship was itself becoming institutionalized as Church structures became more rigidly hierarchical.

, *why* the phenomenon occurred, i.e., what allowed individual Christians to engage in heterosexual friendship, a relationship not normative for the Greco-Roman and Judaic cultures from which the early Christian communities emerged.

Since no culture, or any aspect thereof, develops from a vacuum, the study of a specific cultural phenomenon like friendship demands the painstaking task of reconstructing the social world within which that phenomenon occurs. By the middle of the third century there was enough homogeneity within the Mediterranean area to consider it a Greco-Roman world with identifiable social, political, religious, and economic structures and values. Historians generally agree that the existing thought and behavioral patterns of that time comprised a fairly unified cultural system.[2] Even before the Jewish Diaspora and the Gentile mission which prompted the Christian sect to leap sporadically beyond its Palestinian homeland, early Christian groups were already an integral part of the larger Hellenistic and Roman social world. Their patterns of thought and behavior reflected their involvement within the religious, political, economic, and social world of the Mediterranean.

It is against this background that the circumstances and interplay of forces conducive to Christian friendship must be examined, and the norms for social relationships between men and women be identified. In any established social world there are usually more or less clearly defined areas of space for its inhabitants. These areas are generally designated according to racial, sexual, and social differentiation. Examining the allotted spatial areas of a society can offer important clues about the social relationships, habits, and customs of that culture. The Greco-Roman world (and Judaism by incorporation) was no exception in that sexual differentiation was one of the

---

2. The following studies are particularly useful in tracing the changes occurring during the late second, third, and early fourth centuries. These changes help to identify the reasons for the development of heterosexual friendship within the Christian communities of those same centuries. Cf. Peter Brown, *The Making of Late Antiquity* (Cambridge, Massachusetts: Harvard University Press, 1978); W. H. C. Frend, *Martyrdom and Persecution in the Early Church: A Study of a Conflict from the Maccabees to Donatus* (Oxford: Blackwell, 1965); John G. Gager, *Kingdom and Community: The Social World of Early Christianity* (Englewood Cliffs, New Jersey: Prentice-Hall, 1975); Tom B. Jones, *In the Twilight of Antiquity: The R. S. Hoyt Memorial Lectures* (Minneapolis: University of Minnesota Press, 1978).

important symbols for the maintenance of its world order. Men and women were confined to specific roles according to the established norms of what Fatima Mernissi terms "sexual territoriality," i.e., the separation of male/female space which served as justification for the bestowal or denial of certain privileges.[3] In this way the spatial boundaries served as maintainers of order, and reflected the values the specific culture placed upon the roles allotted to male and female.

The separation of the sexes was effectively accomplished by restricting the space within which each was allowed to function. This imposed a sense of hierarchy which became normative for interpersonal relationships. When the allotted spatial territory was disrupted, the imposed social order was called into question. It was then the function of the guardians of the specific world order either to support and reimpose the social order, or to make necessary changes according to new circumstances. This process of reinstating or selectively reorganizing specific aspects of the established order occurred with a certain regularity during the Greco-Roman world of the third, fourth, and fifth centuries C.E. Thus it is necessary to identify the complex issues and changes that occurred during this period which directly affected the origins and development of new interpersonal male/female relationships.

By the first quarter of the third century C.E. Christianity was "coming of age" within the Greco-Roman world. By then the idea of a canon of New Testament writings was already prevalent and Church leaders found themselves forced into confusing and often unpleasant debates concerning definitions of orthodoxy.[4] In these controversies the Christian writers reflected the prevalent political, religious, and social ferment of the Greco-Roman world.

Though it is true, as Peter Brown states, that "we must be careful to avoid melodramatic insistence on sudden and widespread changes in the climate of religious belief in the Mediterranean world

---

3. Fatima Mernissi, in *Beyond the Veil: Male–Female Dynamics in a Modern Muslim Society* (Cambridge, Massachusetts: Schenkman, 1975), has attempted to reconstruct the factors and circumstances which have brought about significant changes in contemporary male/female relationships in Muslim society. Though I do not agree with several of the basic premises of the study, it offers a valuable methodological approach for such an analysis.

4. See, e.g., *Schism, Heresy and Religious Protest,* ed. Derek Baker (Cambridge: The University Press, 1972), pp. 1–63.

of the second and third centuries," we must be equally aware of the rather abrupt changes brought about by Constantine and Alaric in the fourth and fifth centuries.[5] Religion and religious values could not but be affected by Constantine's invocation of Christianity "as a source of spiritual energy with which to generate social cohesion."[6] Nor could Alaric's sack of Rome in 410 C.E. be dismissed as insignificant when one considers the emotional aftermath of the Visigoths whose influence proved to be more than momentary. The intrusion of new peoples into an already fragmented empire gradually effected dramatic changes not only in the political and economic arenas, but also in people's attitudes and life-styles.

The complex ethnic, religious, and cultural pluralism of the times played a decisive role not only in the establishment, but also in the maintenance of the social world of Christian communities. The reconstruction of this social world within a larger cultural complex calls for a study of the ways in which Christians "saw themselves as a distinct group in society, the ways in which they identified themselves with it—its structures, its values, its culture—and the ways in which they opposed themselves or differentiated themselves from it."[7] Hence, in order to understand the intrusion of heterosexual friendship into the accepted life-style of certain Christians it is necessary to locate its corollaries within the social structures of Greco-Roman society.

Though the paradigmatic role-model for women at this time was the *matrona,* the female head of the household, there were exceptions to the rule. Some women were permitted (though begrudingly) to step outside their allotted space and function on levels not ordinarily accorded to women. Tom Jones, in describing the general characteristics of the fourth century, names several prominent exceptions.

> Again, while one cannot truly characterize a certain trend as woman's liberation, our period was one in which women

---

5. *Making,* p. 8.

6. William A. Clebsch, *Christianity in European History* (New York: Oxford University Press, 1979), p. 87.

7. Robert Austin Markus, *Christianity in the Roman World* (London: Thames and Hudson, 1974), p. 9.

were more prominent in political and intellectual circles than they had been for some time. Among the great women of this era were the unfortunate Hypatia, philosopher, scientist, and mathematician; St. Helena, mother of Constantine, who after a somewhat chequered career became a pillar of the Church; the indomitable Galla Placidia, daughter of Theodosius the Great, who was carried off from the sack of Rome to become the wife of the Visigoth Alaric and later wedded to the pretender, Constantius; Pulcheria, regent for Theodosius II; and Eudocia, the Athenian intellectual who married that same Theodosius.[8]

Jones' examples, with the exception of Hypatia, were women who through marriage to a prominent ruler were allowed greater freedom of mobility beyond the space generally allotted to women. Throughout antiquity a demarcation of racial, sexual, and social roles was a means of establishing one's identity. Diogenes Laertius, for example, attributes to either Thales or Socrates the three blessings for which a man was grateful: "first, that I was born a human being and not one of the brutes; next, that I was born a man and not a woman; thirdly, a Greek and not a barbarian."[9]

But a careful analysis of the legal enactments of the late Roman Republic and the Empire indicate that this sharp role differentiation between men and women was being questioned. Queens and other female members of the upper class often exerted tremendous influence and power, sometimes overshadowing their husbands, fathers, and sons by their shrewdness and courageous tenacity.[10] Under Constantine and other early Christian emperors women won many legal gains in regard to choice of marriage partners, divorce rights, rights

8. *In the Twilight,* p. 5.

9. *Vitae* I. 1, trans. R. D. Hicks. Loeb Classical Library, 2 vols. (London: William Heinemann, 1942), p. 35. Hereafter cited as *Vitae.* Cf. Lactantius, *Div. Inst.* 3.19, who attributes the saying to Plato. The same sentiment is expressed in the Jewish prayer in *Tosefta, Berakot* 7.18.

10. Claude Vatin, *Recherches sur le mariage et la condition de la Femme Mariee a l'Epoque Hellenistique* (Paris: E. de Boccard, 1970); Carl Schneider, *Kulturgeschichte des Hellenismus* (Munich: C. H. Beck, 1967); Charles Seltman, *Women in Antiquity* (London: Thames and Hudson, 1956); K. Thraede, "Frau," *Reallexikon fur Antike und Christentum* VIII, ed. Theodor Klauser (Stuttgart: Anton Hiersehmann, 1972), pp. 197–269.

of inheritance, and greater economic opportunities.[11] The quest for modification of male and female roles was further implemented by the proliferation of philosophical schools, religious associations, and mystery religions. By their emphasis on individual identification with a group of "equals" these schools and groups tended to establish new models for interpersonal relations among their adherents.

Within certain philosophical schools and religious fellowships asceticism, and particularly celibacy, was considered essential for an individual's receptiveness to communication and union with divinity.[12] The motivation for the practice of celibacy was closely aligned to the belief that humans had originally experienced a primordial state of perfection which was forfeited because of a transgression. Celibacy was considered one of the more effective ascetical practices in restoring the individual to the state where communication with divinity was again possible. Therefore the character of celibacy or virginity was "intertwined with the mysteries of the creation, man's primal life in a garden of innocence, and an original transgression."[13] Paul Ricouer summarizes the view which underlay much of the religious thought of both the mystery cults and Christianity in this regard.

> To posit the world as that *into which* sin entered, or innocence as that *from which* sin strayed, or again, in figurative language, Paradise as the place *from which* man was driven, is to attest that sin is not our original reality, does not constitute our first ontological status; sin does not define

---

11. See Gerhard Delling, *Paulus' Stellung zu Frau und Ehe* (Stuttgart: W. Kohlhammer, 1931); J. Donaldson, *Woman: Her Position and Influence in Ancient Greece and Rome and Among the Early Christians* (London: B. Franklin, 1907); John Crook, *Law and Life of Rome* (Ithaca, New York: Cornell University Press, 1967); Johannes Leipoldt, *Die Frau in der Antiken Welt und im Urchristentum* (Leipzig: Koehler and Amelang, 1955); Herbert Preisker, *Christentum und Ehe in der ersten drei Jahrhunderten* (Berlin: Trowitsch and Sohn, 1927).

12. An excellent summary of this is contained in Michel Meslin's "Realities psychiques et valeurs religieuses dans les cultes orientaux" (Ier-Ive siecles), *Revue Historique,* 512 (Octobre–Decembre 1974), 209–314.

13. John Bugge, *Virginitas: An Essay in the History of a Medieval Idea* (The Hague: Martinus Nijhoff, 1975), p. 5.

what it is to be a man; beyond his becoming a sinner there is his being created.[14]

Throughout history this belief in and nostalgia for "return" to a primordial state of innocence and bliss has triggered a variety of myths and rituals of regeneration.

In both the mystery cults and Christianity the perfective attribute of celibacy served as the basic justification for its practice. Abstinence from sexual activity was viewed primarily as acquisition of power and strength rather than negation. Hence Pythagoras may not have had tongue-in-cheek when he responded about the best time to consort with a woman: "When you want to lose what strength you have."[15] Ignatius of Antioch stated a similar view when he extolled virginity as a potent symbol of the strength attainable by the new Christian.[16]

Prior to and contemporary with early Christianity the mystery religions (e.g., the cults of Isis, Cybele, and Mithras) strengthened the view of celibacy as an important cultic approach to the godhead. Michel Meslin demonstrates how within the Isis cult abstinence from food and sexual activity was viewed not as a negation of uncleanness but rather as a means of spiritual conversion.[17] Just as Christian ascetics practiced flagellation and other forms of penance as a means of attaining holiness (i.e., greater access to God), so the followers of Cybele, Isis and other deities inflicted wounds upon themselves during the cultic rituals as a means of access to the divinity. For some, celibacy appeared so essential that self-emasculation was not an uncommon practice.[18]

The majority of recorded instances of amicable relationships between Christian men and women occurred between celibates, i.e., those who chose not to marry or remarry. The motivation for celibacy was generally the pursuit of a "higher" life, i.e., communication

14. *The Symbolism of Evil,* trans. Emerson Buchanan (New York: Harper and Row, 1967), pp. 250–51. Cf. Mircea Eliade, *The Myth of the Eternal Return,* trans. Willard Trask (New York: Harper and Row, 1959), pp. 80–81.

15. Diogenes Laertius, *Vitae* VIII.9, p. 329.

16. *Ep. ad Poly.*

17. "Realities psychiques," p. 293.

18. *Ibid.,* pp. 295–301.

with divinity. Within the Christian communities, to a greater degree than within the mystery cults, those privileged individuals who experienced close communication with and even a sharing in divinity were set apart, beyond and outside the normal structures of society. Peter Brown asserts that this characteristic was unique to the Christians of this period.

> In late antiquity attitudes to culture and society were inextricably intertwined with attitudes to the holy. . . . Unlike paganism and much of Judaism, the Christian communities were prepared to invest individual human beings with supernatural powers or with the ability to exercise power on behalf of the supernatural. It was as precisely identifiable bearers of the holy, and as the heirs of an imagined genealogy of similar bearers of the holy—apostles, martyrs, prophets—that the Christian leaders were able to form the Christian communities. The groups that took up a stance to the society and culture of their times were formed around known revered *loci* of the holy—and these *loci* tended to be human beings.[19]

The wondrous thing was not that these *loci* were human beings but that they included women as well as men, common folk as well as privileged. Within the Christian communities women's aspirations toward and attainment of holiness thereby put serious cracks in the normal spatial confinement of the home. Women who strove for sanctity naturally claimed, in this regard, equality with men. This equality enabled friendship and allowed women an option to that of the Roman *matrona* or head of the household.

But even within this newly acquired and newly legitimated space women were looked after and protected by men who saw their role as one of patron toward client, a prescribed custom of that period.[20] Heterosexual friendships may in fact have been above suspicion

---

19. "Eastern and Western Christendom in Late Antiquity: A Parting of the Ways," in *The Orthodox Churches and the West,* ed. Derek Baker (Oxford: Basil Blackwell, 1976), p. 9.

20. Peter Brown discusses the prevalence of the practice of patron/client in Roman aristocratic society in "The Patrons of Pelagius: The Roman Aristocracy Between East and West," *Journal of Theological Studies,* XXI.1 (April 1970), 56–72.

because they conformed to the socially accepted patron/client relationship.

Peter Brown has described Late Antiquity as a period when changes came about not "as disturbing changes from outside; they happened all the more forcibly for having been pieced together from ancient and familiar materials."[21] This was true in regard to the concept and practice of celibacy in the early Christian communities. Basil of Ancyra was aware of non-Christians' practice of asceticism. He argued that if even good pagans were practicing the ascetic life, the chastity of Christians must exceed theirs.[22] But it is more difficult to locate precedents for the phenomenon of heterosexual friendship since there is an appreciable lack of direct evidence about the practice among non-Christians of the same period.

The most reliable index for identifying the circumstances in Late Antiquity which permitted the practice of heterosexual friendship would be a contemporary pagan's view of the relationship. How would a non-Christian of that period view such friendly extra-conjugal association—as a unique and novel unconvention of still another religious sect? Was there some precedent which bore even a slight resemblance to the phenomenon? A second century Greek medical writer, Galen, deeply impressed by the Christians' ascetical practices, offered the following observation.

> Their contempt of death is patent to us every day, and likewise their restraint in cohabitation. For they include not only men but also women who refrain from cohabitating all their lives; and they also number individuals who, in self-discipline and self-control in matters of food and drink, and in their keen pursuit of justice, have attained a pitch not inferior to that of genuine philosophers.[23]

Galen heads us in the right direction. For him, and presumably many of his contemporary non-Christian observers, Christian men and women ascetics were considered the Christian philosophers of

---

21. *Making*, p. 8.
22. *De Virg.* 67.
23. Richard Walzer, *Galen on Jews and Christians* (London: Oxford University Press, 1949), p. 15.

the era. Just as religion and philosophy were equated in that the goal of each was the attainment of virtues leading to a "higher life," so the ascetic, the "saint" or "holy one" of the Christians, was regarded as an equivalent of the philosopher, the *vir sapiens,* the "wise one." Hence, Plato could speak of a conversion from luxury and self-indulgence to a higher life of contemplation and discipline; the Christian desert-dwellers and monastics extolled the same type of conversion, often with identical Platonic terminology.[24]

Christian hagiography echoed themes found in the various lives of the philosophers.[25] And like the philosophers the ascetics were the marginals of society, existing on the fringes of normative social structures. Hence Brown can speak of the saints of Late Antiquity living in a period when "face and halo tend to come together,"[26] and Nock can depict philosophic "saints of antiquity" living at a time when "around all the prominent figures who founded or developed schools there grew not only anecdotes but also haloes."[27] While to some contemporary observers the philosophers and ascetics were revered as embodiments of divinity on earth, to others they were society's misfits, eccentrics whose vertical relationships with divinity may not have been called into question, but whose horizontal dealings with other human beings often left much to be desired.[28]

If male philosophers and ascetics were considered peripheral, women in those same pursuits must have appeared even more anomalous. For in spite of Roman woman's increased mobility due to legal enactments, her spatial territory was still largely confined to the home. There a sense of hierarchy ruled all of her relationships and behavior. The *matrona* who exercised a degree of independence beyond the norms established became one of the favorite subjects of

---

24. *Repub.* 518.

25. A comparison, e.g., of Christian hagiographical material with Diogenes Laertius' *Lives* of the philosophers shows the recurring themes of miraculous or portentous birth, special aptitudes and abilities, communion with divinity, and supernatural powers such as healing and predicting the future.

26. "Eastern and Western," p. 9.

27. Arthur Darby Nock, *Conversion* (Oxford: Clarendon Press, 1933), p. 1975.

28. Diogenes Laertius, for example, records of Stilpo that "there he would be rambling . . . wasting time in the verbal pursuit of virtue," II.118; or he quotes Alexis speaking about Plato: "You don't know what you are talking about: run about with Plato and you'll know all about soap and onions," and "O Plato, all you know is how to frown with eyebrows lifted high like any snail," III.27–28.

Greek and Roman satire.[29] Any woman who was not in the protective custody of a husband or other male guardian was regarded with contempt and scorn.

However, the exceptions to the rule were more numerous than one might suspect. Diogenes Laertius, for example, lists Lastheneia and Axiothes as two of Plato's and Speusippus' women students.[30] One of the more prominent third century B.C.E. woman philosophers was Hipparchia who, having fallen in love with the lectures and the person of Crates, abandoned all suitors and wealth, adopted male attire, and "went about with her husband and lived with him in public and went out to dinners with him."[31] When accosted by another philosopher whom she had outwitted she said, "Do you suppose that I have been ill-advised myself, if instead of wasting further time upon the loom I spent it in education?"[32]

Porphyry tells how Plotinus, because he was considered "a holy and god-like guardian," was entrusted not only with the education of many younger boys and girls, but also with women who were greatly devoted to him: "Gemina, in whose house he lived, and her daughter, Gemina . . . and Amphiclea, who became the wife of Ariston son of Iamblichus, all of whom had a great devotion to philosophy."[33]

But perhaps the most notable of the women philosophers of the late fourth to early fifth centuries C.E. was Hypatia, an outstanding teacher and writer at Alexandria, who, according to Socrates, surpassed all the philosophers of her own time.[34] Synesius of Cyrene, who credits her with his lifelong interest in science and philosophy, revered her as the genuine leader of the rites of philosophy.[35] For Hypatia philosophy was a way of life spent in the pursuit of perfection, a pursuit which demanded celibacy. Like her, many Roman noblewomen were attempting to achieve a similar goal through a life of

---

29. William Chase Greene, in *The Achievement of Rome: A Chapter in Civilization* (New York: Cooper Square, 1973), pp. 96–105, discusses the censure due to any *matrona* not following the accepted norms.

30. *Vitae* IV.1, p. 375.

31. *Vitae* VI.7, p. 101.

32. *Idem.*

33. *Life of Plotinus* 9, in *Plotinus,* trans. A. H. Armstrong, Loeb Classical Library, Vol. I (London: William Heinemann, 1966), p. 31.

34. *Hist. Eccl.* VII.5.

35. *Ep.* 137.

Christian asceticism. Palladas' epigram on Hypatia could as well refer to any of the increasing number of Christian women ascetics.

> Revered Hypatia, ornament of learning, stainless star of
> wise teaching, when I see you and listen to your discourse,
> I worship you, looking on the starry house of the virgin; for
> your business is in heaven.[36]

Even after Synesius became a Christian, his admiration for and friendship with Hypatia remained constant. His seven letters to her are clear examples that many concepts of virtue and the good life were the same for Christians and non-Christians alike, at least among the better educated classes. Hypatia's brilliant career ended in martyrdom. For reasons unknown some riotous Christians abducted her, took her to a church, and there dismembered her body with sharp tiles and burned the pieces.[37] It seems plausible that her popularity and renown, her charismatic leadership, and her reputation for classical learning exacerbated the resentment society may have felt toward a woman who was engaging in such "unwomanly" exploits.

For Hypatia and her ascetic counterparts celibacy was essential in the pursuit of wisdom and perfection. The spatial confinement of the family system was no longer adequate and celibacy offered a release in the form of a viable option. This option legitimated the creation of new space necessary for women's access to non-familial endeavors. Within this new space women were able to transform certain social structures such as social relationships between men and women. Christian literature of the third through the fifth centuries demonstrates the impact that celibacy had upon the formation and nature of heterosexual friendship. Synesius of Cyrene observed that those elected by providence to pursue wisdom were brought together in a very special friendship.

> Whenever I recall our association in philosophy ... I attri-
> bute our meeting to God, our guide. For nothing less than
> a divine cause could compel me. ... And if human affairs

---

36. *Greek Anthology* III, trans. W. R. Paton, Loeb Classical Library (Cambridge: Harvard University Press, 1968), p. 202.

37. Socrates, *Hist. Eccl.* VII.5.

join together in mutual sympathy those who share them in common, divine law demands that we who are united through the intellect, the best thing within us, should honor one another.[38]

Mutality of goals as the basis for true friendship was a recurring theme in the Christian writers' depictions of heterosexual friendship. The common sharing of the search for external order and inner harmony served to minimize the restraints of sexual differentiation prescribed by societal structures. This minimization of sexual segregation allowed the development of a new paradigmatic relationship other than the conjugal one. Heterosexual friendship between celibates emerged as the Christian corollary of the husband/wife, patron/client paradigm.

The following chapters identify those changes within the Greco-Roman culture which allowed the paradigm shift. Just as the patriarchal family ultimately served as a model for Church structure so the husband/wife relationship provided the background against which the new friendship paradigm developed. Hence the accounts are projected against the broad background of accepted social relations as normatively experienced within the family structures.

In locating the particularities of the paradigm shift primary sources from a variety of literary genres have been selected. The depictions were carefully chosen so as to include as wide a range as possible from the geographically diffuse and culturally diverse Christian communities. The chapter headings were suggested by the texts themselves according to the existential situation of the individual and/or groups whose friendships were there recorded. Hence, after a general review of male/female social relations in Greco-Roman and Judaic societies, and a brief appraisal of those early Christian beliefs and practices which allowed for changes in interpersonal relationships, successive chapters deal with the nature and characteristics of heterosexual friendship as depicted in the accounts of Christian martyrdom, *syneisaktism* ("spiritual marriage"), and communal asceticism.

---

38. *Ep.* 137.

CHAPTER TWO

Normative Greco-Roman and Judaic Male/Female Relationships

In classical Jewish and Greco-Roman literature the most notable instances of deep personal relationships are those between man and man—e.g., David and Jonathan, Orestes and Pylades, Damon and Pythia, Achilles and Patroclus. Although there is an occasional mention of amiabilities between women (e.g., Ruth and Naomi) there are few either general or specific allusions to friendship between man and woman. In examining the literary works of these cultures for indications of attitudes toward and practice of types of friendship the researcher needs to determine the correlation between the literary utterances and a people's lived responses. The most the historian can claim is that the material reflects theories and moral principles taken for granted by the more highly articulate individuals of a certain period. It is equally difficult to evaluate to what extent an author accepts or rejects the tenets and practices of a specific society. Hence, the lack of explicit literary references to a thing is no proof of its non-existence within society. In attempting to establish correct interpretations, the painstaking efforts of locating and interpreting implicit evidence is often more productive than the explicit reference. The present study is a case in point. Though there is no formal treatise written between the second through the fifth century C.E. about heterosexual friendship as here defined, Christian literature of that period is rich with clues about the nature, cause, and actual practice of that friendship. Classical literature of Jewish and Greco-Roman cultures remains, for the most part, devoid of such clues on the subject.

Attempting to assess the practice of friendship as evidenced in the literature of the Jewish people presupposes an awareness of the fact that this included not only the inhabitants of Palestine but those segments of the Jewish populace scattered throughout the Greco-Roman and Oriental world.[1] Although the laws, interpretation, and opinions of Jewish life and conduct recorded in the Hebrew Bible and the Talmud (body of Jewish civil and canonical law) were the accretions of many centuries, for the diverse Jewish communities of the Diaspora they provided an essentially harmonious expression of a distinctive value system. Neusner marshals evidence that the pervasive and universal presence of the Torah (the Hebrew Bible and the body of teachings and opinions on Jewish laws and customs) allowed the diverse Jewish communities to be legitimately characterized as a distinctive civilization among other societies.[2]

A classic example of friendship in the Hebrew Bible is that between David and Jonathan.[3] The rabbis interpreted this relationship as an illustration of love which was everlasting in that it did not depend on any ulterior motive such as money, praise, or prestige.[4] The closest approach to a biblical instance of friendship between women is that between Ruth and Naomi, though it was basically a relationship dependent upon a sense of duty rather than affection.[5] In both instances, however, friendship existed between persons of the same sex. In the Judaic culture, as in the Greco-Roman, known instances

---

1. For an analysis of the enormous complexities of the political and religious scene in the world of Judaism during this time, see Morton Smith, "Palestinian Judaism in the First Century," in *Israel: Its Role in Civilization,* ed. Morton Davis (New York: Harper and Row, 1956), pp. 67–81; George Foot Moore, *Judaism in the First Centuries of the Christian Era: The Age of the Tannaim* (Cambridge: Harvard University Press, 1927); Jacob Neusner, *From Politics to Piety: The Emergence of Pharisaic Judaism* (Englewood Cliffs, New Jersey: Prentice-Hall, 1973); Gerd Theissen, *Sociology of Early Palestinian Christianity,* trans. John Bowden (Philadelphia: Fortress, 1978).

2. Neusner, *Understanding Rabbinic Judaism from Talmudic to Modern Times* (New York: KTAV, 1974), p. 5. Cf. Markus, "The Achievement of Hellenistic Judaism," in *Great Ages and Ideas of the Jewish People,* ed. Leo W. Schwarz (New York: Modern Library, 1956), pp. 123–28.

3. I Samuel 18–20. Unless otherwise stated the Old and New Testament translations are those of the Jerusalem Bible (Garden City, New York: Doubleday and Company, 1966).

4. Avoth 5:16.

5. Ruth 1.

of close friendships between men and women were exceedingly rare, presumably on the grounds of sexual morality. The recorded instances of male–female relationships (e.g., Adam and Eve, David and Bathsheba, Samson and Delilah, Judith and Holofernes) dramatize the view of woman as source of evil and cause of man's downfall, a notion not compatible with the practice of friendship based on equality. Consequently, the maxims and exhortations regarding friendship precluded the notion of women's potential for friendship with men.

There are many allusions to the value of friendship in the historical books of the Bible and the pithy sayings and maxims of Wisdom and Rabbinic literature.[6] The Hebrew Bible, in fact, by considering human friendship symbolic of the intimacy between God and humanity, added a dimension and dignity not accorded friendship in the Greco-Roman tradition. The Greeks in particular conceived of divinity as an object of dim and distant speculation, whereas the Jewish concept was that of an all-powerful yet gracious divinity who was on fairly friendly terms with certain leaders such as Abraham and Moses.[7] St. George Stock maintains that the possibility of a friendly God–man relationship "never entered the mind of a thinker like Aristotle, who held that friendship is destroyed when persons are separated by a wide inequality; and therefore between God and man, or personalties so far removed from one another, friendship or intercourse was not conceivable."[8] The fact that the Jewish concept of God as patriarch implicitly equated divinity with maleness widened the chasms of inequality both between divinity and femaleness *and* between male and female, thus disallowing friendship between men and women.

Since the majority of recorded instances of friendships within the Jewish communities are those of biblical, rabbinic, and Hasidic heroes, women would by societal strictures be disqualified from mention. The Hebrew Bible recounts the deeds of strong heroic women like the prophetesses Miriam and Huldah, the national saviors Judith and Esther, the judge Deborah, and the proselyte Ruth. The leadership roles of these women suggest that in the very early period of

---

6. E.g., Prov. 13:20; 17:17; 3:12; Eccl. 6:7, 14, 17; Avoth 2:9; 1:6; Makkot 10a.

7. E.g., Exodus 12, 15, 17, 33.

8. "Friendship," *Encyclopedia of Religion and Ethics,* VI (New York: Scribner, 1914), p. 132. Cf. Aristotle, *Nic Ethics* VIII.7.

Jewish history sex roles were not as differentiated as they became later. But the bulk of Jewish literature viewed woman as a secondary creature created as man's helpmate, a view which served to justify and reinforce the separate and unequal roles for men and women in Jewish culture. The oft-quoted rib/apple/serpent myths became effective symbols for sanctioning the view of woman's subordination. Woman's divinely instituted and prescriptively regulated purpose was to bear and rear children in the fear of Yahweh, and to provide a home-atmosphere conducive to her husband's position as master and family interpreter of the Torah. If there were any role which accorded to woman the honor and status accorded the male, it was the role of mother, a role which confined her, however, to the strict confines of the home.

Both by law and custom Jewish women were excluded from the privileges and the responsibilities of religious life.[9] Only the male was God's spokesman and the legal heir of the Jewish name and tradition. Women could not be members of a minyan (the quorum of ten required for public worship), and were permitted neither to read from the Scroll of the Torah nor to lead the prayer service. They performed no public congregational function and had to sit in a separate section in the synagogue.[10] They were neither admitted as witnesses in court nor allowed an active or passive vote since this would be tantamount to conceding them authority in public office. A law recorded in Deuteronomy allowed a man to divorce his wife, but the wife had no such right.[11] In a number of later enactments some of these discriminations were either diminished or prevented, but the changes toward a more humane development of law proceeded too slowly to ensure the coincidence of law and custom.[12]

---

9. Three useful references for an historical survey of women in the Jewish tradition are Phyllis Bird, "Images of Women in the Old Testament," in *Religion and Sexism: Images of Woman in the Jewish and Christian Tradition,* ed. Rosemary Radford Ruether (New York: Simon and Schuster, 1974), pp. 41–88; Collins, *A Different Heaven,* pp. 47–136; and Gail B. Shulman, "Women from the Back of the Synagogue: Women in Judaism," in *Sexist Religion and Women in the Church: No More Silence,* ed. Alice L. Hageman (New York: Association Press, 1974), pp. 143–65.

10. Megillah 23a.

11. Deut. 24:1–4.

12. E.g., the institution of ketubbah, the marriage contract, demanded a settlement by the groom so that in the event of divorce or death his wife would be provided

For whatever reason and by whatever means the subordination of women was effectually institutionalized, it remained a reality of Jewish existence which obstructed the free flow of communication and friendship between men and women. The rabbis argued that by excusing women from the difficult and time-consuming performance of the precepts of the Torah, they would be free to give their undivided attention to the equally necessary and sacred tasks of the home. The roles were considered complementary in that the man was to provide for the family financially and actively preserve the religious values and beliefs of the Torah; the woman was to maintain the home and teach her children true values and the right way of life.

Though she was deprived of many legal rights, woman as helpmate and bearer of new life was relatively well protected by law and tradition. She benefited likewise from the healthy puritanism of the Jewish life-style and the close-knit bonds of family, the general excellence of parental relations, reverence for elders, and stern but loving upbringing of children. In her role as mother and wife she was generally highly respected, and it is within the established bonds of marriage that the closest Jewish approximation of heterosexual friendship occurred. However, the restraint imposed by the legalistic concept of covenant and the detailed prescriptive priorities ensuring its maintenance did not allow for extensive commentary or freedom of expression about those aspects of culture generally taken for granted. Since celibacy was uncommon and considered an unnatural way of life, and since married women were consistently throughout Jewish culture confined rather strictly to the home, there was no opportunity for heterosexual friendship to develop outside marriage.

The most explicit references to friendship in Greek and Roman literature are found in general discussions on friendship as an integral part of various systems of philosophy. Philosophical works, however, are generally not the best indicators of *wie es eigentlich gewesen ist,* particularly in the case of Greek philosophy which relegated friendship primarily to the public, political sphere of life. Consequently, the topic appears most frequently in treatises dealing with important political phenomena.[13] Already in the society of the Ho-

___

for. Also, later legislation allowed that in certain instances the wife could institute divorce proceedings.

13. Major treatments of the topic are found in the philosophical works of Plato,

meric poems friendship denoted not so much a relationship based on deep ties of affection, but rather a reciprocal agreement to lend support and to be supported whenever the demand arose.[14] It was in a sense an instrumental type of friendship, a *quid pro quo* or *do ut des* type of relationship as distinguished from the expressive, emotive, or transcendent relationship considered basic to close personal relationships. Friendship at this stage of Greek history appears as an extension of family and kinship ties to include wider social relationships. Even in instances of apparent personal friendships such as that between Achilles and Patroclus, the relationship may well have been founded to support one another in various enterprises.[15] Another aspect of friendship as an extension of familial ties is that of guest-

---

Aristotle, Cicero, Plutarch, and Epictetus. Horst H. Hutter has analyzed the major Greek and Roman treatises in "Friendship in Theory and Practice: A Study of Greek and Roman Theories of Friendship in Their Social Settings," Diss. Stanford University, 1972. Hutter maintains that the Greco-Roman concept of friendship as the major principle in terms of which political theory and practice were described, explained, and analyzed has been supplanted in the modern world by the idea of market exchange as the major principle for the intellectual ordering of the political world. Although his study has no direct bearing on heterosexual friendship as here defined, his conclusions corroborate the view that women's participation was either very restricted or non-existent. One has to beware, however, of assembling disparate quotations from various contexts. A text which serves as a corrective to the generally negative interpretation of women in Greece and Rome is W. Den Boer, *Private Morality in Greece and Rome: Some Historical Aspects* (Leiden: E. J. Brill, 1979), pp. 242–271. Since the text deals exclusively with the position of women in marriage, Den Boer does not speak to the issue of heterosexual friendship except as he reiterates the view here presented— that the paradigm for male/female relationship was that of husband/wife, and that women's influence was exerted "from the living room and not in a public place" (p. 250).

14. The Greek word *philos* (most frequently translated "friend" or "someone" or "something dear or precious") and *philia* ("friendship") are the words generally used in Greek literature to describe the friendship relationship here discussed. A problem, of course, arises in the interpretation of the words as they are variously used in the texts. The Greek word *philos* appears possessive in origin, since one finds it applied in both the *Iliad* and the *Odyssey* to such diverse objects as country, parts of the body, clothing, wife, child (*Iliad* I.20; II.261; III.31; VII.130; *Odyssey* V.493; etc.). One needs to be very conscious therefore that the value-aspect or meaning of such value-words like love, friendship, friend, etc., differ in emotive power, connoting different qualities and gradations of intensity; further, that the value terms may have a variety of meanings depending upon their position on the value-scales of different individuals, groups, and societies. For a general analysis of this problem and specific examples from Greek literature see K. J. Dover, *Greek Popular Morality in the Time of Plato and Aristotle* (Berkeley: University of California Press, 1974), pp. 1–45.

15. Homer, *Iliad* I.307.

friendship which united houses with ties of hospitality so binding that even the normal enmities of war could not sever the bond.[16]

The closest approximation to heterosexual friendship appears in the fifth century B.C.E. in the maxims attributed to Pythagoras. Although there is much uncertainty about Pythagoras and his school of followers there is evidence that he formed a religious association which purported to live together as a community of friends, shared all things communally, and sought a certain kind of religious perfection, intellectual advancement, and human comradery.[17] The four major maxims attributed to Pythagoras illustrate a deep concern for and understanding of friendship as communal experience, and became four of the basic precepts of the Pythagorean school: (1) friends share in the perfect communion of a single spirit;[18] (2) friends share everything in common;[19] (3) friends are equals and friendship is an indication of equality;[20] (4) a friend is a second self.[21] It is difficult to establish the extent to which these precepts were actually practiced within the school. The members did put all their possessions into a common stock but, as Ferguson argues, the sharing concept undoubtedly varied at different periods in the history of the school.[22]

---

16. In the *Iliad* VI.215–35, Homer portrays the opponents Glaucus and Diomedes renewing the ties of hospitality and the promise of friendship after discovering that their fathers were sworn guest-friends. They dismounted on the battlefield, clasped hands, and exchanged armor so that all present would recognize their claim to be guests and friends from the time of their respective fathers.

17. Cf. Iamblichus V, *Life of Pythagoras,* and Plato, *Republic* X.

18. References located in Aristotle, *Nic Ethics* IX.8 and *Eud. Ethics* VII.6; Cicero, *De Amicitia* XXI.81 and *De Officiis* I.56.

19. Diogenes Laertius, *Lives of Eminent Philosophers* VIII.10; X.11; Plato, *Lysis* 207; Aristotle, *Nic. Ethics* VIII.9; *Eud. Ethics VII.2; Cicero, De Officiis* I.51; and Terence, *Adelphia* 803ff.

20. Diogenes Laertius, VIII.10; Aristotle, *Nic. Ethics* VIII.5 and IX.8.

21. Aristotle, *Nic. Ethics* VIII.3, Plutarch, *Moralia* II, and Cicero, *De Amicitia* XXI.8, refer to a true friend as "another self."

22. John Ferguson, *Moral Values in the Ancient World* (London: Methuen, 1958), p. 55, suggests that the later replacement of the early Pythagorean arithmetical equality by a geometrical equality of proportion justified distinctions within the community. It seems plausible that as the school opened its membership to people of different social classes, members of the upper strata of society maintained their autonomy and prestige within the structure by retention of their personal holdings. Wayne A. Meeks, in "The Image of the Androgyne: Some Uses of a Symbol in Earliest Christianity," *History of Religions,* 13 (February 1974), p. 172, argues that though there were women in the old Pythagorean community, the general role depicted was the conventional one. He maintains that only in the Epicurean "Garden" were women

The organization of the order, its theory of friendship as equality, and its universalistic attitude toward admission into the society all came into conflict with the traditional mores of society and elicited strong opposition from the aristocratic segment.[23]

In an age characterized by extreme inequality of the sexes the Pythagorean fellowship was unique in its implications that there were no significant differences between men and women. According to its admission policy at least, both men and women were welcomed on an equal footing. It is unfortunate that there is no literary indication of the degree of congruence between policy and practice, but both precedent and subsequent literature suggest that female equality with the male was not one of the permanent vestiges of Pythagorean influence. Diogenes Laertius states that influential Pythagorean communities were established in southern Italy and that the contact with these communities gave Plato the idea of the academy.[24] There is no question of the Pythagorean influence upon later fellowship groups, particularly the Stoics and the Epicureans, some of whose concepts found expression in the practices of the early Christian communities.

Friendship is a pivotal concept in the two great philosophical systems of Greek thought, the Platonic and the Aristotelian. Granted that philosophic systems are not as a whole the most accurate indices of reality, still these two systems are relevant to this study because of the light they shed on new developments of the concept of friendship. Within the context of the Platonic *Dialogues,* for example, there appears a new concept in the valuation of friendship, the concept of love of wisdom as friendship's guiding value. For Plato love or desire (*eros*) is the motive force of friendship, the lowest form

---

fully equal. Women's participation in certain activities and their friendships with men within the Pythagorean groups, however, seems to indicate that women's roles in these communities extended beyond the conventional ones.

23. Polybius, *Histories* II.39, indicates that around the middle of the fifth century there were many bitter attacks on the society.

24. Diogenes Laertius, VIII.3. Ferguson, p. 55, states that not only was Plato influenced by their system, but that in some sense "Pythagoras' maxims upon friendship formed the ultimate inspiration of the public school and the residential university." There is no doubt that the Pythagorean Order attained lasting significance by providing an organizational model for later philosophic schools. The Academy, the Lyceum, the Stoic School, and the Epicurean Garden followed the Pythagorean experiment in basing their internal structure on the maxims of friendship. The members of these schools were known as *philoi,* or "friends."

being expressed in sensuality, and the highest in love of wisdom, truth, and beauty.[25] Friendship is only possible among the good since only a good man inspired by his love for wisdom can both be and have a friend. The highest ideal then for human relationships is to stimulate each other by sharing in the common aspiration toward wisdom. This relation may start from physical attraction since such attraction is part of the aspiration toward beauty, but it can ultimately surpass the merely physical or sexual love. Plato's friendship is, according to Diotima in the *Symposium,* essentially non-physical. However, it is not an absence of appreciation of the physical, but its sublimation, a notion frequently reiterated by later theorists, including early Christian writers. Ferguson maintains that some of the genius of Plato's scheme of *eros* and *philia* lies in the fact that it "offers a purposive direction for life and a healthy basis for human relations in terms of a power which is cosmic in scope and yet relevant to the human heart."[26]

As for woman's participation in the relationships discussed in the *Symposium,* she is allowed an inferior or base type of friendship very similar to that enjoined upon her later in the *Nichomachean Ethics.*[27] This base or sensual type of relationship had no spiritual or intellectual content, implying that the objects of such a relationship were capable of functioning merely as biological machines or had not yet reached the level of maturity necessary for participation in noble or true friendship.

In Books 8 and 9 of the *Nichomachean Ethics* Aristotle presents what is the fullest and most systematic treatment of friendship extant in classical literature.[28] For him friendship is a liberating force which

---

25. Plato's most complete analysis of friendship is contained in the *Symposium,* but the dialogues *Lysis* and *Phaedrus, The Laws,* and the *Republic* contain insights into the practical aspects of some of the theories. It is sometimes difficult in Plato's works to distinguish between *eros* and *philia,* since both at times signify love, but only *philia* refers to love among friends. *Eros* is generally used in the *Symposium* while *philia* occurs regularly in the other dialogues.

26. Ferguson, pp. 92–93.

27. Plato, *Symposium* 181, 182, and Aristotle, *Nic. Ethics* VIII.7.

28. One of Aristotle's successors, Theophrastus, also wrote an important monograph on friendship. With Aristotle's work this served as model for later schools of thought, particularly the Epicurean and Stoic. Although the treatise has not survived, it was the major source of Cicero's *De Amicitia* or *Laelius,* and Plutarch's short trea-

extends from its origins in kinship to the wider realm of society, and thence to the whole human race. It has the capacity to perfect the individual who will then, along with other good or perfected men, help to shape and maintain the state in such a way as to ensure justice in its dealings and stability in its organization. This relationship between the life of the individual and the well-being of the community or state became a common theme incorporated into the beliefs of such fellowship groups as the Stoics, Epicureans, and early Christian communities.

Aristotle's theory of the state as a friendship community is notable for its emphasis on the need for reciprocity, promotion of another's good for his sake, desire for another's safety, pleasure in another's company, the view of a friend as "another self," and in general for its altruistic directedness. As a universal theory, however, it is defective because of its aristocratic and male exclusiveness. For example, in Aristotle's analysis of the three types of friendship, that based on pleasure, on utility, and on virtue or goodness, only the third is considered true friendship, that "between good men who are alike in excellence and virtue."[29] Although the word *anthropoi* ("men") can be used in the generic sense, it generally referred to adult males who were full-fledged citizens. Women were thus automatically eliminated from participation in the highest or true type of friendship.

Aristotle includes women in this discussion of friendship between unequals, and since the previous section deals with equality as the basic constituent of true friendship Aristotle is implicitly stating his belief in women's incapacity to be true friends.[30] He asserts that since friendship is an association or community, friends naturally aim at living together and sharing such common experiences as drinking, playing dice, sports, hunting, and study of philosophy, all of which remained the exclusive domain of the male.[31] His view that choice of one's friends was a prerequisite of true friendship implies

tise on friendship, *Moralia* 93A–97B. For an excellent summary and analysis of classical theories of friendship, see Ludwic Dugas, *L'Amitie Antique* (Paris: Felix Alcan, 1914).

29. Ostwald, *Nic. Ethics* VIII.3, p. 219.
30. *Ibid.*, VIII.7, pp. 227–28.
31. *Ibid.*, IX.12, pp. 271–72.

that husband and wife were ineligible for such friendship, since husband and wife generally had no voice in choice of partner.

Aristotle did allow, however, that friendship between husband and wife could bring "both usefulness and pleasantness with it, and if the partners are good, it may even be based on virtue or excellence."[32] The implication is that it would rarely, if ever, occur. This view of the inequality of woman, who is considered servile by nature, is systematically developed by Aristotle in his writings on the subject of biology and the political sciences. In these works the free Greek male represents reason which, because of its capacity for rule, must subjugate the corporeal elements of society represented by women, slaves, and foreigners.[33]

Literary works of other classical Greek philosophers, poets, and playwrights corroborate the view that friendship consisted primarily in relationships between men. There is no appreciable evidence that friendship crossed sexual lines, and in fact the literary articulations about hostility toward women indicate the social atmosphere of at least certain segments of society.[34] The notable exception in this general pattern is that of the *hetaerae,* female companions, courtesans, of whom Aspasia (friend of Pericles) is the most brilliant example.[35] The *hetaerae* were not only expected to be faithful lovers, but also convivial, intellectual companions equally conversant in both the practical and the theoretical issues of the day.

The *hetaerae,* however, seemed in most ways to be trained to think and act like men so that they did not fit the general pattern of

---

32. *Ibid., Politics,* IX.15, p. 239.

33. Aristotle, *Politics* I.102; *On Generation of Animals* I.729b; II.731b, 737a, 738b. Cf. Plato, *Timaeus* 91.

34. Dover, pp. 95–102, discusses samplings of Greek literary evidence on hostility toward women and suggests reasons for the prevalence of such feelings. It is important, however, neither to overemphasize nor to deemphasize this aspect since it is fairly easy to be selective in one's choice of evidence. The problem is not that of having too many conflicting sources, but of finding enough sources which might speak to the issue of women in Greek and Roman society.

35. Not to be confused with the *hetaery,* or "union of friends," a close-knit association or union of men based on similarity of age and social class. It was probably one of the strongest of Greek social institutions, providing for its members various activities which helped form closer and more intimate bonds than those supplied by the Greek family. For descriptions of these groups, see George Miller Calhoun, *Athenian Clubs in Politics and Litigation* (Austin: University of Texas Bulletin, 1913) and Hutter, pp. 165ff. and 188–90.

life of Greek women, and a reason men may have sought their companionship was precisely that they were different from other women. Hutter claims that their differences "served to mute and overcome male anxiety and hostility toward women which were dominant in other contexts of relatedness."[36] The important position they assumed in the social life of Athens, especially after the Peloponnesian War (431–404 B.C.E.), is evidenced in the later writers of Attic comedy whose plots frequently included the adventures of a *hetaera.* Since by custom respectable women and girls were barred from the society of men, the *hetaerae* were the female element represented in that society. Although they did enjoy a freedom generally denied to Greek women, the demands of their occupation and the fact that they were in a sense public servants of male society did to some extent circumscribe their mobility and freedom.

The Stoic school, like the Pythagorean fellowship, extended the concept of friendship from a particularistic, exclusive relationship to a universal, all-inclusive principle of the brotherhood of all mankind. Within its system friendship extended from the polis to humanity at large, and the concept of *philia* was broadened to include *philanthropia,* a "doing good" to others. In this extension of love for mankind in general *philia* was deprived of its exclusive character. And since friendship was considered a relationship of inner equality which was externally demonstrable certain groups ruled that there should be no external demonstration of differences between social classes or sexes.[37]

The Epicurean school viewed friendship as an exclusive bond between individuals who had the same aspirations and ideals. For the members *philia* was no longer an adhesive force binding together the citizens of the state; instead it was a substitute for political involvement which might interfere with a person's striving for *ataraxia,* freedom from concern. Theoretically, the critics of Epicurus and his school who claim that his system is based on egocentricity are correct in that the root motive of Epicurean friendship was self-interest.[38] The fact remains, however, that the Epicurean schools' practice

---

36. Hutter, p. 232.

37. See Ferguson, pp. 70–71, for a record of Epicurus' sentiments on friendship.

38. E.g., Lactantius, *Inst. Div.* III.17. For a more detailed analysis of women's role in the Epicurean community, see Meeks, pp. 172–74.

exhibited a type of friendship which was based on concern for one another. In the Garden all distinctions were to be dropped. As in the case of the Stoics the community included adults and children, men and women, slaves and free. Like the Jewish Essenes and Christian monastic communities of a later period, the members withdrew from society not in order to escape responsibility, but to espouse something which to them appeared a better cause. Although it is difficult to estimate the extent to which equality for all was actually practiced, for society at large there appeared no radical change in the social structure. The fact, however, that at least some of the members of Greek and Roman societies were allowed the experience of living the ideals of friendship in community indicates one of the needs of societies of the time and points to the fact that friendship both in theory and in practice was encompassing a broader spectrum of humanity.

Cicero borrowed many of his views from both Stoic and Epicurean doctrines. His treatise on friendship, *De Amicitia* or *Laelius,* is derived for the most part from selections from Greek philosophy. There is an important change, however, in Cicero's theory of friendship in that it signifies a break with the dominant Greek conception of politics as the arena for friendship. This undoubtedly occurred because Cicero was not a part of a smaller political unit like the Greek *polis,* but a citizen of an expanding empire whose equally expansive problems included an increase in political alienation. His work reflects the withdrawal of virtue from the public realm into the private, personal sphere. Living in a period in Roman history which witnessed the gathering of many diverse cultures into one political enclave, Cicero, like Cato, mourned the disappearance of many former ideals and concepts, one of which was equality in political friendship. Hence, theories of friendship increasingly stressed withdrawal of the phenomenon from the public, political sphere into the private, personal one. This is not surprising in an age which witnessed greater emphasis on personalism and a growing sense of individualism.

But in spite of this, within both the Jewish and the non-Jewish Hellenistic cultures, women in general were confined to the restrictive territoriality of home and hearth which allowed no real opportunities for participation in heterosexual friendship. Though by the first century C.E. women had legally acquired certain social and moral rights which set them above their Greek women contemporaries, they were still generally regarded as instruments of men's pleasure.[39] They were confined to their own space, separated from men by a rigid division of labor, fewer educational opportunities, and exclusion from such things as religious cultic practices, rites of initiation, and social rewards. Women were conspicuously absent from events and occasions which would allow for the expansion of intellectual energies. They were important in the home and their position within the family may have been more active than the extant Greco-Roman literature reveals, but, except in the rare instances of royalty and the *hetaerae,* women were prohibited from the arena of action where people exchanged ideas and expanded intellectual, social, and cultural horizons.[40] And since it was in a climate of mutual interaction and exchange that friendships could originate and flourish, women's exclusion from these areas eliminated, or at best minimized, the possibility of heterosexual friendship within Judaic and Greco-Roman societies.

---

39. A study by Charles Winick, *The New People: Desexualization in American Life* (New York: Pegasus, 1968), implies that part of the blame for the fall of Rome must extend to Roman women who, in his view, demanded more from life than subordination to husbands. Although he admits that no single cause entirely explains Rome's decline, he overemphasizes the extent to which Roman women's legal gains caused a sexually blurred culture, and hence a breaking down of the system. Cf. K. Thraede's summary of the role and status of women during this period, "Frau," *Reallexikon Fur Antike und Christentum,* VIII, ed. Theodor Klauser (Stuttgart: Anton Hiersemann, 1972), 197–269.

40. Sarah B. Pomeroy, in *Goddesses, Whores, Wives, and Slaves: Women in Classical Antiquity* (New York: Schocken Books, 1975), pp. 149–89, demonstrates that the Roman *matrona* had more access to money and power and experienced deeper marriage relationships than her Greek counterpart. This apparently allowed for an occasional eruption of the *matrona*'s spatial territoriality, but not to the degree that friendship between men and women became a culturally accepted phenomenon for many.

CHAPTER THREE

Early Christian Themes:
Unity and Reconciliation

No new movement, religious or otherwise, is created *ex nihilo.* There are always borrowings or carry-overs from the existing culture, the continuation of those traditionally accepted ideals, values, and customs which are still deemed either necessary to or compatible with the present structures of society. But there are also new emphases and the incorporation of new insights, ideas, and practices responsive to the particular group's objectives. New religious movements, sects, or cults frequently arise because the members perceive a world-view somewhat different from that of the culture which up to that point nurtured and sustained them.[1] Consequently, some of the traditional views and customs no longer deemed plausible are ultimately discarded for those more compatible with the people's new needs and aspirations. Heterosexual friendship, it is here argued, was one of the new ideals which became possible within early Christian communities.

There is no dearth of evidence that heterosexual friendships existed, but the reason for the expansion of the paradigmatic husband/ wife relationship is not so easily discerned. In order to ascertain *why* this specific phenomenon was able to develop within early Christianity it is necessary to reconstruct the world of the early Christians, attempting to discover the Christians' own understanding of them-

---

1. Peter Berger describes the process of change which generally occurs when new values replace the old, in *The Heretical Imperative: Contemporary Possibilities of Religious Affirmation* (Garden City, New York: Doubleday, 1979), pp. 26ff.

selves and their world. Jonathan Z. Smith maintains, "Once an individual or culture has expressed its vision of its place, a whole language of symbols and social structures will follow."[2] Hence, one must first discover what the Christians' vision of "their place" was, and then attempt to discern what it felt like "to live in a world described and determined by the symbols, rituals, and language of early Christianity."[3] While it is beyond the scope of the present study to reconstruct every aspect of early Christian society, it is essential to recognize those aspects which relate more directly to changes in interpersonal relationships.

Although it is difficult to assess the degree of correlation between the theoretical views expressed in a people's literature and the daily lived-out experiences of those people, the literary reiteration of specific themes and ideals indicates certain value-invested priorities. The New Testament as "the book" of the early Christians grew out of the needs and aspirations of the emerging communities and reflected their view of reality. Hence, recurring motifs suggest those values and ideals which became prominent and even normative for the communities which helped shape "their book." John G. Gager, in a study of the social world of early Christianity, asserts that when new religions work toward the creation of new worlds,

> . . . old symbols are given new meanings and new symbols come to life; new communities define themselves in opposition to previous traditions; a new order of the sacred is brought into being and perceived by the community as the source of all power and meaning; new rituals emerge to remind the community of this sacred order by creating it anew in the act of ritual celebration.[4]

If there is any one theme which looms large in the extant literature of the early Christian communitites, it is that of "newness"—

---

2. "The Influence of Symbols upon Social Change: A Place on Which to Stand," *Worship,* 44.8 (October 1978), 469.

3. Jonathan Z. Smith, "The Social Description of Early Christianity," *Religious Studies Review,* 1.1 (September 1975), 21.

4. *Kingdom and Community: The Social World of Early Christianity* (Englewood Cliffs, New Jersey: Prentice-Hall, 1975), p. 11. Cf. Peter Berger's theories of "world construction" and "world maintenance" in *The Sacred Canopy. Elements of a Sociological Theory of Religion* (Garden City, New York: Doubleday, 1969).

newness of creation, of life, of the spirit, of the mind, etc., concepts
which both empowered their world and gave it meaning by compar-
ing/contrasting it with an "old" or prior value system. The very title
of the Christian communities' book, the *New* Testament, indicates
the Christians' conscious definition of themselves in opposition to
the Jewish people and the religion which had previously nurtured
and sustained many of them. According to the author of the Epistle
to the Hebrews the old law of the Jewish religion and its command-
ments were abrogated for the new: "The earlier commandment is
thus abolished, because it was neither effective nor useful, since the
Law could not make anyone perfect; but now this commandment is
replaced by something better—the hope that brings us nearer to
God."[5]

In the New Testament writers' visions of a new world taking
shape, Christ is seen as the initiator par excellence of a new order: "If
anyone is in Christ, he is a new creation; the old has passed away,
behold the new has come."[6] The new order is variously conceived as
"new heavens and a new earth," a "new Jerusalem," a time for "all
things being made new," "new wine" (not to be stored in old bot-
tles), and "new doctrine."[7] The Christians saw themselves as "a chosen race, a royal priesthood, a consecrated nation, a people set apart
. . . the people of God," who individually and corporately exhibited
"new life," "new spirit," and "newness of mind."[8] The descriptive
phrases describing the new people were taken directly from the Hebrew scriptures' descriptions of the Jews' relation to Yahweh.

Christ as the direct source of the new creation is consistently
contrasted with specific prototypes found in the Hebrew scriptures.
By contrast Christ not only emerges superior to the old (as one who

---

5. Heb. 7:18–19. Cf. Jn. 13:34 and 1 Jn. 2:8. Although it can be argued that the
views expressed in the New Testament were those solely of the individual writers, the
fact that they became part of the official canon by the fourth century indicates their
importance in sustaining the Christians' world view.

6. 2 Cor. 5:17. Cf. Gal. 6:15.

7. 2 Pt. 3:13; Apoc. 21:1–2 and 3:12; 2 Cor. 5:17; Mt 9.17; Lk. 5:37–38; Mk.
1:27; Acts 17:19–20; Mk. 16:17; Rom. 6:4. In the New Testament both *neos* and *kairos*
are used for "new," though *neos* is the less common. For a linguistic analysis of the
distinctions see *Theological Dictionary of the New Testament*, ed. Gerhard Kittel,
Vols. III and IV (Grand Rapids, Michigan: Wm. B. Eerdmans, 1967), 447–454 and
896–901.

8. 1 Pt. 2:9–10; Col. 3:10; Rom. 6:4, 7:6, and 12:2.

completes or fulfills), but personifies the ultimate perfection of the various types. He is the mediator of the New Testament, the model for a new and living way, the cornerstone, the high priest of the order of Melchizedek who replaces the old Levitical priesthood, and the last Adam.[9] According to the author of Hebrews Christ "has been found to deserve a greater glory than Moses" in that Moses was merely a servant of Yahweh while Christ was Yahweh's son.[10] In the Gospels Christ's shedding of his "blood of the covenant" becomes the source of the Christians' new life, symbolically renewed in the Eucharistic ritual.[11] Several patristic writers, in fact, distinguished the Christian community as a *new* or *third* race, set apart from and superior to both Jew and Gentile.[12]

The concept of the Christians' "newness" served both to differentiate and to separate Christians from their non-Christian compatriots (like virtue from vice, light from darkness, etc.) but it also established a powerful image for unity among the Christians themselves.[13] The new message was one of reconciliation, the Christians first being reconciled with Christ and consequently serving as ministers of reconciliation to each other and the world.[14] Paul, in particular, speaks of the Christians' "oneness in Christ" as the most reliable index of reconciliation. He reminds the Christians in Galatia that their promise of salvation was contingent not upon ethnicity, social status, or sexuality, but upon their reconciliation with and acceptance of Christ who made them one.[15]

This unitive aspect, based on Christ's intimate relationship to his followers, was expressed in the New Testament by the vine/branches, head/members, and cornerstone/temple metaphors.[16] The Christians' belief in reconciliation with God and with each other was reiterated by such phrases as "one body, one spirit," "one Lord, one

---

9. Heb. 9:15 and 10:20; 1 Pt. 2:4; Heb. 5:10, 6:20 and 7:18; Rom. 5:14–15; 1 Cor. 5:21 and 45–47; Jn. 19:5.

10. Heb. 3:3–6.

11. Mt. 26:28 and Mk. 14:24.

12. Tertullian, *Ad Nat.* 1.8 and *Apol.* 42; Eusebius, *Hist. Eccl.* 1.4; and *Preaching of Peter.*

13. 2 Cor. 6:14–16.

14. 2 Cor. 5:18–19.

15. Gal. 3:28. Cf. 1 Cor. 12:13–27; Col. 3:10; Eph. 6:8.

16. Jn. 15:1–5; 1 Cor. 12:12–27; 1 Cor. 3:11–12; 1 Pt. 2:6–7.

faith, one baptism."[17] The emphasis was not on those elements within society which divided or differentiated, but on the unique role the Christians posited for Christ as exemplar and model of unification and reconciliation between races, social classes, and the sexes.

Edmund R. Leach, in a myth analysis derived in part from C. Levi-Strauss, explains how such reconciliation between elements within a society can occur. He states, "In every myth system we will find a persistent sequence of binary discriminations as between human/superhuman, mortal/immortal, male/female, legitimate/illegitimate, good/bad ... followed by a 'mediation' of the paired categories thus distinguished."[18] The early Christians' recorded stories and anecdotes about Christ present him as one whose mediation between humanity and divinity likewise mediated such binary oppositions as those described by Paul:

> All baptized in Christ, you have all clothed yourselves in Christ, and there are no more distinctions between Jew and Greek, slave and free, male and female, but all of you are one in Christ Jesus.[19]

The male/female set of paired categories is particularly significant for the study of the development of heterosexual friendship. Wayne Meeks argues convincingly that the elimination or minimization of the binary opposition, male/female, was part of a larger movement within early Christianity which stressed unity through unification of opposites,[20] He demonstrates how the Christian modification or elimination of the generally accepted male/female differentiation served in early Christianity as a prime symbol of salvation and allowed for certain new ideals and practices. Paul's reminder that in Christ there is no more distinction between Jew and Greek, slave and free, male and female, is seen by Meeks as part of the bap-

---

17. Eph. 4:4–6. Cf. Phil. 1:27 and 1 Cor. 12:13.

18. "Genesis as Myth," in *Myth and Cosmos,* ed. John Middleton (Garden City, New York: Natural History Press, 1967), p. 4. Myth is here defined as the expression of a concept basic or essential to a people's belief system.

19. Gal. 3:28.

20. "The Image of the Androgyne: Some Uses of a Symbol in Earliest Christianity," *History of Religions,* 3 (February 1974), 165–208.

tismal ritual used at that time. As such it reminded both the newly baptized and the Christian community present of Christ's reconciliatory role in unifying the members of his "body." The conviction that all Christians were part of the one "body of Christ" was an important symbol which the Christians cherished and cultivated from early times, and which probably played a greater role than any other symbol in helping to construct the Christian world-view. The fact that the human body was a common denominator accessible and comprehensible to everyone undoubtedly explains the symbolic importance allotted to it.

Though Meeks concludes that for Paul the male/female reconciliation referred chiefly to "spiritual equality" (i.e., equal access to salvation) with no radical changes in social or political status for women, his insight on the way in which reunification language and symbol can function within a community has implications for the present study.

> There is reason to believe that the symbolization of a reunified mankind was not just pious talk in early Christianity, but a quite important way of conceptualizing and dramatizing the Christians' awareness of their peculiar relationship to the larger societies around them. At least some of the early Christian groups thought of themselves as a new genus of mankind, or as the restored original mankind.[21]

And just as the Christians reconciled the Jew/Gentile dichotomy by the notion of a "third race" (*tertium genus*), they likewise mediated the slave/free, male/female categories by the notion of themselves as an extended Christian family. This is evident in their use of familial terminology and practices.

The notion of Christians as family is reiterated in the theme of brotherhood and sisterhood in Christ. New Testament literature suggests that whatever differentiations may have separated individuals prior to baptism, their adoption into God's family and their acceptance of Jesus as brother was intended to minimize such separa-

---

21. Meeks, p. 116.

tions.[22] Christians exhorted each other to "love the brotherhood" and to "let brotherly love continue," and they addressed each other in the familiar and almost formulaic "brothers and sisters" in Christ.[23] John, for example, wrote to seven churches in Asia: "My name is John, and through our union in Jesus, I am your brother and share your sufferings, your kingdom, and all you endure."[24]

In the first Christian generation dogmas and institutional structures did not dominate the scene as they did in later periods. Meeting in private homes the early Christians "broke bread together" and exchanged the familial kiss of peace in a table fellowship which both produced a cohesive unity and provided meals for the needy, thus minimizing the distinctions of wealth and social class.[25] According to Acts, many early Christians considered it not only appropriate, but even essential, to hold everything in common, for "they sold their goods and possessions and shared out the proceeds among themselves according to what each one needed."[26] The early Christians' ritual initiation through baptism, the memorial fellowship of the common meal, the appellation of "brothers and sisters," the kiss of peace, and the sharing of material resources indicate the seriousness with which these Christians considered themselves a community of Christ's body. John Gager argues that the Christians' radical sense of community was one of two distinctive factors facilitating the ultimate triumph of Christianity over its competitors.

---

22. Gal. 3:28. Cf. Mk. 3:35 and Mt. 12:50 where Christ considers anyone who does the will of God as "my brother, and sister, and mother."

23. 1 Pt. 1:22, 2:17 and 3:8; 2 Pt. 1:7. Cf. 1 Tim. 5:1–3.

24. Rev. 1:9.

25. For a study of the complex relationship between the more familial agape feasts and the Eucharist see Josef A. Jungmann, *The Mass: An Historical, Theological, and Pastoral Survey* (Collegeville, Minnesota: Liturgical Press, 1975); Leonel L. Mitchell, *The Meaning of Ritual* (New York: Paulist, 1977); Gregory Dix, *The Shape of the Liturgy* (Westminster, England: Westminster, 1945); Willy Rordorf, *et al., The Eucharist of the Early Christians,* trans. Matthew J. O'Connell (New York: Pueblo Publishing Company, 1978).

26. Acts 2:45. Cf. Acts 4:32–37 and 5:1–11 which record the punishments of Ananiaes and Sapphira who kept part of the proceeds of their property sale. See also Martin Hengel, *Property and Riches in the Early Church: Aspects of a Social History of Early Christianity* (London: SCM Press, 1974) and L. William Countryman, *The Rich Christian in the Church of the Early Empire: Contradictions and Accomodations* (New York: Edwin Mellen Press, 1980).

From its very beginning, the one distinctive gift of Christianity was this sense of community. Whether one speaks of "an age of anxiety" or "the crisis of the towns," Christian congregations provided a unique opportunity for masses of people to discover a sense of security and self-respect.[27]

While the Christians' communal organization as the body of Christ played a crucial role in Christianity's ultimate survival and success, the founder-figure, Jesus, appears in early Christian literature as the source of legitimation for the communities' existence. It is the Christians' being "clothed" in Christ which distinguished them from others and removed the social, racial, and sexual barriers of society in preparation for the final days of the "new creation."[28] The Gospel accounts depict Jesus as an advocate of social change, particularly in the area of respect for individuals. He appears as one sent to call the poor, the handicapped, the sinner, and women to the freedom and equality of the kingdom of God. He initiates a movement toward greater personalism and acceptance of individuals by calling his followers not "servants" but "friends."[29] Jesus' general attitude as recorded indicated his concern for the integrity of the individual not on the level of abstraction, but in the person of a sister or a brother.

That Jesus' friendship extended to women as well as men is evidenced by the Synoptic accounts of Jesus making his way through towns and villages accompanied by the twelve "as well as certain women" mentioned by name, "and several others who provided for them out of their own resources."[30] As for Jesus' more personal relations to specific women, one need only recall his recorded friendships with certain women followers, particularly Mary Magdalene and Martha. Both Luke and John attest to Jesus' close relationship with them, and the Gnostic *Gospel of Philip* ascribes a privileged position to Mary Magdalene: "There were three who always walked with the Lord: Mary his mother and her sister and Magdalene, the one who

27. *Kingdom and Community,* p. 140.

28. Gal. 3:24–26. Cf. 1 Cor. 12:27; and 2 Cor. 5:17.

29. Jn. 15:15.

30. Lk. 8:1–3 and Mt. 27:55–61. Women were likewise present at Jesus' death, and were the first witnesses to his resurrection. Cf. Lk. 23:49–55 and 24:1–11; Mk. 16:1–11; Mt. 28:1–10; Jn. 20:11–18.

was called his companion."[31] According to the Gnostic text, Jesus'
special love for Mary Magdalene evidently was a source of envy and
consternation for some of the disciples, for they asked Jesus, "Why
do you love her more than all of us?"[32]

Jesus' attitude toward women as recorded in both the New Testament and the Gnostic sources is one of positive identification with
women as the equals of men. He respected his many women followers and close, personal women friends to the point of deliberately vi-
olating certain accepted social mores. Two instances in particular
stand out as examples of Jesus' awareness of unjust elements within
his society in regard to women; the story of the woman caught in
adultery and that of the Samaritan woman at the well. The former
demonstrates Jesus' rejection of the double standard of sexual morality, whereby this woman was to be punished for her participation in
the adulterous act, while the man was not accused. After Jesus called
into question the male-accusers' sinfulness, no stone was cast. Jesus
did not condemn the woman, but encouraged her to sin no more.[33] In
the second narration Jesus again acted in a highly unconventional
manner, for not only did he speak openly with a woman stranger, but
as a Jew he asked to drink from the ritually unclean bucket of a Samaritan.[34] Respect for the integrity of an individual superseded the
demands of the law and social custom. Leonard Swidler maintains
that the Jesus of the Gospels was a true feminist, in that nowhere
does he display the generally negative attitude toward women that
was prevalent in Palestine.

The fact that the overwhelming negative attitude toward
women in Palestine did not come through the primitive
Christian communal lens by itself underscores the clearly

31. *The Nag Hammadi Library*, ed. James M. Robinson (San Francisco: Harper
and Row, 1977), pp. 135–136, hereafter cited as NHL. Cf. Lk. 10:38–42; Jn. 11:1–44
and 12:1–8; Mk. 14:3–9; Mt. 26:6–13.

32. *Gospel of Philip*, NHL, p. 235. Cf. *The Dialogue of the Savior* which includes
Mary Magdalene as one of three chosen to receive special teaching.

33. Jn. 8:3–11.

34. Jn. 4:1–42. For further interpretations of Jesus' relations toward women, see
Evelyn and Frank Skagg, *Women in the World of Jesus* (Philadelphia: Westminster,
1978), pp. 102–160, and Elisabeth M. Tetlow, *Women and Ministry in the New Testament* (New York: Paulist, 1980).

great religious importance Jesus attached to his positive attitude—his feminist attitude—toward women; feminism, that is personalism extended to women, is a constitutive part of the Gospel, the Good News, of Jesus.[35]

The motif of reconciliation or mediation of the opposites, male/female, occurs in several Gnostic texts dealing with the image of the androgyne (that which has both male and female characteristics). Although these texts were not incorporated into the official New Testament canon and the Gnostic Christian groups were eventually considered heretical, the frequency of the androgyne motif indicates the importance allotted to the theme of reconciliation.[36] The *Apocalypse of Adam,* for example, describes androgyny as an achievement to be attained, while the *Exegesis on the Soul* considers it the original condition of the soul.[37] The *Gospel of Philip* describes original humanity as an androgynous being living in harmony. The "fall" occurred when male and female were separated and death came into being. In order to overcome death humanity had to recover its original androgyny.[38]

The *Gospel of Thomas* has Jesus explaining that only through mediation of the male and female could salvation be acquired: "When you make the male and the female one and the same, so that the male not be male nor the female female . . . then you will enter the Kingdom."[39] In the same gospel, when a rather prejudiced Peter complains, "Let Mary leave us, for women are not worthy of Life," Jesus chides Peter for his negative attitude toward woman: "I myself shall lead her in order to make her male, so that she too may become a living spirit resembling you males. For every woman who will make herself male will enter the Kingdom of Heaven."[40] Instead of seeing Jesus in this instance corroborating Peter's view of women as inferior and unworthy of salvation, it appears more in keeping with

35. "Jesus Was a Feminist," *Catholic World* (January 1971), 177–183.

36. For an elaboration of the gnostic views on the androgyne see Elaine Pagels, "The Gnostic Vision," *Parabola* 3.4 (November 1978), 6–9.

37. NHL, pp. 256–257 and 181.

38. NHL, p. 141.

39. NHL, p. 121. Cf. *The Dialogue of the Savior* where Jesus has come "to destroy the works of femaleness," p. 237.

40. NHL, p. 130.

other recorded depictions of Jesus to interpret this as a reassurance that his message was able to overcome even the prevalent prejudice against women.

The *Gospel of Mary* advocates an attitude of acceptance toward women based on Jesus' respect for them. In the account Peter asks Mary to share with the disciples the Savior's words which she alone knew. After Mary complied, Peter questioned whether Jesus had really revealed these things to Mary and "not openly to us? Are we to turn about and all listen to her? Did he prefer her to us?" To this Levi replied:

> Peter, you have always been hot-tempered. Now I see you contending against the woman like the adversaries. But if the Savior made her worthy, who are you indeed to reject her? Surely the Savior knows her very well. That is why he loved her more than us.[41]

The male/female reconciliation is further expressed in certain Gnostic descriptions of God as both male and female, both Father and Mother.[42] The *Apocryphon of John* interprets the Trinity as "I am the One who is with you always; I am the Father; I am the Mother; I am the Son."[43] According to Irenaeus, a second century critic of certain Gnostic groups, one of the Gnostic teachers named Valentinus imaged a dyadic god: "The Primal Father" and the "Mother of the All."[44] Although virtually all feminine God-imagery was rejected by the orthodox Christian tradition, the fact remains that some early Christian groups translated the Christian message of reconciliation and unity into terms which included positive male and female aspects in defining human nature and the nature of God.[45]

---

41. NHL, p. 473. For an analysis of the conflict between Peter and Mary see Pheme Perkins, *The Gnostic Dialogue: The Early Church and the Crisis of Gnosticism* (New York: Paulist, 1980), pp. 131–141.

42. See Pagels, "The Gnostic Vision," p. 8–9 and *The Gnostic Gospels* (New York: Random House, 1979), pp. 50–58.

43. NHL, p. 99. Cf. *Trimorphic Protennoia,* pp. 462–467 and the *Gospel of Thomas,* pp. 128–129.

44. *Adv. Haer.* 1.11. Cf. Hippolytus, *Ref.* 6.18.

45. For the status of women in certain early Christian communities (many subsequently viewed as heretical) see Elisabeth Schüssler Fiorenza, "Word, Spirit, and

In conclusion, the early Christian records of Jesus' open attitude toward women and his close relationships with individual women was a positive force in allowing changes in male/female relationships. The generally accepted bipolarization of the two sexes allowed for little communication between non-married men and women. The Jesus of the Gospels and certain Gnostic texts advanced the notion of complementarity of the sexes and allowed for a restructuring of social norms so as to include mutual male/female relationships of support and respect outside the marriage bonds. Heterosexual friendship was one of the early Christians' subjective responses to the reconciliatory emphasis of their new world view, a "new heaven and earth." The notion of the Christians' "oneness in Christ," exemplified in Jesus' recorded attitude of acceptance of and empathy with his followers and friends (man, woman, slave, free, rich, poor, Jew, Gentile) paved the way for an irruption of those boundaries which normally restricted communication between people. It now remains to examine how, after the majority of Christian communities reverted to a less egalitarian stance around the year 200, heterosexual friendship remained as a new paradigm of male/female relationships.

Power: Women in Early Christian Communities," in *Women of Spirit: Female Leadership in the Jewish and Christian Traditions,* eds. Rosemary Ruether and Eleanor McLaughlin (New York: Simon and Schuster, 1979), pp. 39–70.

CHAPTER FOUR

Martyrdom

One of the literary genres of early Christianity which most graphically demonstrates the particularities of male/female friendships is that of the *Acta Martyrum*, anecdotal narrations about the experiences of individuals and groups about to die as martyrs for the Christian faith. The problematic of using the martyr-accounts as depictions of interpersonal heterosexual friendships lies in the uniqueness of the martyrdom experience, i.e., it represents an atypical existence. When people are united by a common belief in the divinity of an exemplar or model for their own existence, there is already a certain minimization of social, racial, and sexual factors which normally prohibit dialogue and interpersonal communication. And when a group's loyalty to its religious founder and exemplar demands imprisonment and the prospect of imminent death, that prison community further dispenses with the normative racial, sexual, and social differentiations. Death does, indeed, become the great leveler.

In spite of the accounts' presentations of atypical existence they are here included because of the insights they offer on the motivations for the practice of heterosexual friendships. The instances of sexual egalitarianism within prison communities reflect some basic assumptions about women and indicate how these assumptions were able to be transcended by certain beliefs of the early Christians.

In the Christian communities of the first three centuries the martyrs stood head and shoulders above the general Christian populace. These individuals were conspicuous for their loyalty to a common faith in Jesus of Nazareth, their Messiah, and common hope in their union with that Messiah through resurrection after death. The stories of these individuals and groups, narrated in the *Acta Martyrum,* are an extensive body of literature recounting the arrest, imprisonment, trial, and execution of Christians from the earliest times through the reign of Diocletian (284–305).[1] The narrations range from first person and eyewitness accounts to imaginative fiction, all of which were to serve as sources of edification and exhortation for the readers and listeners. For the contemporary historian they provide the necessary documentation for reconstructing the world of the martyr.

The documentation must, however, be viewed against the cultural crisis which provoked martyrdom. The multiple aspects of the crisis are generally subsumed under the term "persecution." Although it is outside the scope of this study to deal with the complex issues of origins, intensity, and geographic extension of the persecution, it is necessary to determine what factors in society provoked its possibilities.[2]

The early Christians were Jews whose new faith in their proclaimed Messiah, Jesus of Nazareth, still maintained a continuity with the Jewish faith of their fathers. Consequently the civil authorities in both East and West did not always clearly distinguish between Jews and Christians, a coincidence which easily allowed the transfer of Jewish/Greco-Roman hostilities to the Christians as well. And like the Jews, the Christians were enthusiastic about proselytism which, if too successful, posed a threat to social and religious institutions of the Greco-Roman classical world.[3] Many Christian martyrs

---

1. The most recent edition of twenty-eight of the most authenticated *acta* is that of Herbert Musurillo, trans, and ed., *The Acts of the Christian Martyrs* (Oxford: Clarendon, 1972). Throughout this chapter the parenthetical numbers refer to pages in Musurillo's book, hereafter cited as *Acts.*

2. In what is probably the most definitive recent study of persecutions in the early Church, W. H. C. Frend, *Martyrdom and Persecution in the Early Church: A Study of a Conflict from the Maccabees to Donatus* (Oxford: Basil Blackwell, 1965), traces the development of persecutions from the Hellenistic East where the Jews were persecuted before the Romans or Christians appeared on the scene. Frend deals specifically with the issue of the relation between Jewish and Christian persecution by civil governments in "The Persecutions: Some Links between Judaism and the Early Church," *Journal of Ecclesiastical History,* 9 (October 1958), 141–58.

3. This view is expressed by Tacitus, *Histories,* V.5.2. In many of the martyr accounts, the same view is expressed by the civil interrogator who accuses the Chris-

were undoubtedly their own worst enemies in that their articulated equation of powers of evil with contemporary secular authorities further aggravated already tense situations.[4]

That some Christian groups had acquired a recognizable identity distinct from the Jews and other religious cults is evidenced by their appellation, the "third race."[5] This corporate identity incurred the suspicions that minority groups commonly arouse. Among the accusations made against the Christians was that of disloyalty, i.e., disruption of state-harmony by spreading atheism. In the eyes of their critics the Christians "while living as members of a community . . . deliberately rejected the gods on whom the prosperity of that community rested. In addition . . . they refused to give even nominal recognition of Caesar as lord by swearing on his genius."[6] These charges often provoked official proceedings against the Christians.[7]

However varied and complex the cultural crisis which evoked martyrdom, the actual martyrdom accounts ascribe one motive for the Christians' acceptance of the phenomenon, the martyrs' personal identification with the martyr/exemplar, Christ. Both the *Acta Martyrum* and related literature reflect the views and attitudes which inspired such identification.

The term "martyr" connotes "a witnessing" or "confessing," and in the Christian context the meaning was extended to include the concrete, personal identification with Christ, the one confessed or witnessed to. But at least one group of martyrs differentiated the reality of "martyr" and "confessor." The writer of the second century

---

tians of being atheists because of their refusal to pay homage to the gods of the state or the genius of the emperor. Cf. the martyrdom accounts of *Polycarp, Carpus,* and the *Martyrs of Lyons,* in *Acts,* pp. 5, 25, 73.

4. Cf. *Acts,* pp. 63, 71, 129, 155, 219.

5. Tertullian, *Scorp.* 10.

6. Frend, "The Persecutions," p. 155. The following include a variety of interpretations of this complex issue: David Daube, *Civil Disobedience in Antiquity* (Edinburgh: University Press, 1972); Eric R. Dodds, *Pagan and Christian in an Age of Anxiety: Some Aspects of Religious Experience from Marcus Aurelius to Constantine* (Cambridge: The University Press, 1968); Simeon L. Guterman, *Religious Toleration and Persecution in Ancient Rome* (London: Aiglon, 1951); Jacques Moreau, *La Persecution du Christianisme dans L'Empire Romain* (Paris: Presses Universitaires de France, 1956); Donald W. Riddle, *The Martyrs: A Study in Social Control* (Chicago: University of Chicago Press, 1931).

7. Late in the second century, e.g., Celsus accused the Christians of setting up a wall between themselves and the rest of mankind; Origen, *Contra Celsum* VIII.2.

account of the *Martyrs of Lyons* tells how in spite of the martyrs' imitation of Christ by suffering various tortures, they nonetheless refused to be called martyrs and chided those who insisted on doing so.

> For it was their joy to yield the title of martyr to Christ alone, who was the true and faithful witness, the first born of the dead. . . . And they would recall the martyrs that had already passed away, saying: "They were indeed martyrs, whom Christ has deigned to take up in their hour of confession, putting his seal on their witness by death: but we are simple, humble confessors" (83).[7a]

Death alone advanced the witnessing Christian from confessor to martyr. And it is in the anticipation of that advance as portrayed in the *Acta* that one can best understand the attitude and behavior of the witnessing community.

The martyrdom accounts reflect conditions conducive to the establishment of egalitarian attitudes and practices. This is not surprising since a group's self-identification as something different from the rest of society generally minimizes or even eliminates distinctions within the group. The martyr's special identification as sharers in the suffering, death, and resurrection of Christ is emphatically expressed in the various depictions of the martyrs' beliefs and activities. The *Acta Martyrum* indicate that the anticipatory resurrected life after death was the organizational principle of the communities. The emphasis was not on dying but on the resurrection promised by the already resurrected martyr/exemplar, Christ.

So strong was the martyr's sense of identification with Christ that the martyrs felt an alleviation of pain due to Christ's participation in their suffering. Felicitas, for example, groaning in childbirth, was taunted by a jailer who queried how she could possibly suffer martrydom when she could scarcely endure childbirth. She responded that the present suffering was her own, whereas in the arena Christ within would bear the suffering for her (123, 125). This sense of identification with the martyred Christ recurs as a basic motif within the *Acta*.[8]

7a. See footnote 3, pp. 45–46.
8. E.g., *Acts,* pp. 3, 73, 235. Cf. Eusebius, *Hist. Eccl.* 5.1.23.

There is no dearth of women martyrs in this early period of Christian history when sporadic persecutions brought to trial members from various Christian communities. Women appear as both equals and leaders among those whose confessing to the name of Jesus had its effect on the communities at large. The depictions demonstrate how communal witness to belief in Christ was both supported by and supportive of close, interpersonal relationships among those who anticipated imminent entrance to eternal life. Although the purpose of the accounts (to exhort and provoke emulation) to a certain extent dictated the content, the narrations provide ample evidence that the prison communities experienced a degree of male/female, free/slave equality unknown or not recorded outside these confines. Several of the accounts demonstrate more explicitly than others the disruption of normative relationships so as to include male/female friendships.

One of the most dramatic recountings of confrontation between a populace, its provincial administration, and local communities of Christians is that of the *Martyrs of Lyons.* Preserved in Eusebius, the account purports to be a letter from the Christian churches of Lyons and Vienne to the churches in Asia and Phrygia.[9] It offers a harsh portrait of an anti-Christian uprising in Gaul under Marcus Aurelius in 177. The instigators of the anti-Christian demonstrations were immigrants from Asia Minor whose actions resulted in the banishment of Christians from public places and their eventual imprisonment and execution.

Four of the captured Christians were for some reason particular targets against which the angry crowd and prison officials vented their hatred and anger. Among these was Blandina, a slave girl whose exploits warranted the extended introduction in the text, "Blandina, through whom Christ proved that the things that men think cheap, ugly, and contemptuous are deemed worthy of glory before God, by reason of her love for him which was not merely vaunted in appearance but demonstrated in achievement" (67). Whether Blandina's being a woman, a slave, or both, elicited her being consid-

---

9. *Hist. Eccl.* 5.1–3. See *Acts,* pp. 62–85. Frend, *Martyrdom and Persecution,* pp. 1–30, analyzes the texts to confirm his claim that the problem the Christians posed to the Roman Empire was fundamentally that posed by Judaism, namely the claims of theocracy versus those of a world empire.

ered somewhat of a marvel, the text clearly indicates that for the martyrs, identification with Christ was the source of their strength, love of God their motivation, and action rather than intent the ultimate test of both.

Throughout the account Blandina maintains a privileged position among her prison-peers. In what appears as a type of martyrdom-marathon, she surpasses the expectation of her mistress and peers, surfacing as leader in a reversal of established roles (67–81). Though considered inferior on at least three counts (she was a slave, a woman, and supposedly physically weak) she so courageously withstood the various tortures that she ultimately outranked the free, the men, and the strong. The narrator supplies the reason for her endurance: ". . . tiny, weak, and insignificant as she was she would give inspiration to her brothers, for she had put on Christ, that mighty and invincible athlete . . . and through her conflict had won the crown of immortality" (75).

The account's portrayal of the group's solidarity and the members' individual concern for each other is undoubtedly due in part to the exhortatory nature of the narration, and in part to the unusual and even unnatural circumstances of prison confinement. But beyond those factors there is another which more adequately explains the strong bonds of unity and equality expressed in fellowship and friendship within the community. The imprisoned members of the "Christian brotherhood," as the narrator described them, shared a common faith in God and particularly in Christ as martyr/exemplar, a common hope in the promise of immortality, a common adversary in the devil, and a common need to be supportive of each other in their individual and communal confessions. Mutuality of goals served as a powerful force for unification rather than a polarization of opposites. The martyrs' communal identity is further expressed by the members' addressing each other with the familial "brother" and "sister," terms by their nature non-discriminative and devoid of hierarchical overtones (75, 79).

Other martyrdom accounts portray groups experiencing the same egalitarianism productive of heterosexual friendship. How much of this may be due to the consideration of Christians as the "third race" is difficult to ascertain. Though the pagans' shouts of "away with the third race" were intended to be anything but complimentary, for the Christians the distinction of being set apart may well have allowed them more freedom from the general social conventions of their times.[10] However, according to the evidence of the accounts, the Christians' awareness of their positive identity as imitators of Christ provided the basic validation for equality of members.[11] In the *Testament of the Forty Martyrs of Sebaste* for example, the "prisoners of Christ" remind the communities outside the prison of the true nature of their Christian fellowship.

> For the invisible God is revered in our brother whom we see; and though this saying refers to our true brothers, the meaning is extended to all those who love Christ. For our God and holy Saviour declared to be brothers not those who shared a common nature, but rather those who were bound together in the faith by good deeds and who fulfill the will of *our Father who is in heaven* (359).

The martyrs' staunch belief in God as Father and Jesus as Brother pervades the exhortatory and consolatory accounts, and the communal witness to that belief in no small way contributed to the egalitarian nature of the martyrs' prison-communities.

The story of Sabina, a slave girl martyred during the Decian persecution, testifies to the way in which many of the heterosexual friendships may have been formed. Angry that Sabina had become Christian, her mistress had her bound and placed on the mountainside. Pionius and fellow Christians rescued her, however, and were attempting to have her freed from the control of her mistress. As a priest who had a certain amount of authority within the community and who had taken up Sabina's cause, Pionius was undoubtedly greatly esteemed by her, an esteem which with the passage of time and greater familiarity evolved into a close, personal friendship.

Since Sabina spent the greater part of her time at the house of Pionius, she was arrested along with him and three of his companions. As the prisoners were being taken to jail, some of the bystanders, noticing that Sabina was clutching Pionius' clothing, jested,

---

10. See Tertullian, *Scorp.* 10.
11. Cf. *Acts,* 4, 17, 35, 69, 75, 83, etc.

"Why, how terrified she is that she may be weaned" (149). When later asked whether she could not have died in her own city, she retorted, "What is my native city? I am the sister of Pionius" (159).[12] It is plausible that women converts like Sabina felt a special attraction for those in priestly ministry, particularly if they had been instrumental in their conversion or instruction. And the fact that priests, by virtue of their function as official communicators with and transmitters of divinity, were looked upon as unique, the "holy ones" of the Christian community, may have initiated and legitimated the practice. Agathonice, for example, after witnessing the death of her teachers, Bishop Carpus and a deacon, Papylus, entrusted her children to God and followed the martyrs in death after telling the proconsul, "If I am worthy, I shall eagerly desire to follow the footsteps of my teachers . . . this is what I have come for, and this is what I am prepared for, to die for Christ's name" (35).[13]

Even in those martyrdom narratives devoid of explicit indications of heterosexual friendships, the evidences of respect, concern, and affection of the members for each other intimate that such relationships were a common experience of the members. That such relationships were sometimes questioned is obvious in Chariton's response to the magistrate who intimated that her affiliation with the male martyrs sullied her reputation: "Rather I have become God's servant and a Christian, and by his power I have kept myself pure and unstained by the taints of the flesh" (57). There is the charming but pathetic story of Potamiaena whose almost instant friendship with Basilides, the guard who led her to execution, seemed to continue after her death. To the amazement of his acquaintances, Basilides at one point had to admit that he was a Christian. He was consequently imprisoned and beheaded, but only after revealing to his Christian brothers that Potamiaena had appeared to him after her execution informing him that she had requested the Lord for his conversion, had received her request, and would be seeing him shortly. The narrator adds that Potamiaena effected other such conversions

---

12. Sabina may have said this to avoid recognition by her former mistress. For that reason Pionius had earlier advised that she call herself "Theodote" rather than "Sabina" (147).

13. Cf. the instructor/catechumen friendship-development between Perpetua and Saturus (107–31).

by appearing to people in their sleep (133, 135).

One of the most descriptive accounts of the martyrdom process is the *Martyrdom of Perpetua and Felicitas.* The narrative is particularly relevant to this study in that its descriptions of the prisoners' sayings, visions, and prison activities reflect the aspirations and hopes of a community whose personal bonds of friendship are clearly manifested.

The account is a firsthand one, the basic sections of which are recorded in the persons of two of the martyrs, Perpetua and Saturus, while a redactor (possibly Tertullian) supplies the introduction and conclusion.[14] That both Perpetua's and Saturus' accounts are authentic self-descriptions seems confirmed by the fact that they differ markedly from each other's and from the redactor's style and use of language. The majority of historians who have seriously studied the issue have accepted the claim of Perpetua's and Saturus' authorship, and the veracity of the redactor.[15]

We learn from the account that six friends were arrested in Africa during the persecution under Septimius Severus in 202–3. They were Vibia Perpetua, daughter of a wealthy provincial, who emerges from the text as leader of the group; her slave, Felicitas, who was eight months pregnant; Saturus, already a Christian and the instructor of the others; Revocatus, Saturninus, and Secundulus, three catechumens. The five recently instructed converts were baptized while under surveillance by the authorities and were jailed a few days later along with their instructor.

---

14. The Latin original consists of twenty-one sections with four basic divisions:

Sections 1–2	Introduction by a redactor, possibly Tertullian.
Sections 3–10	Perpetua's prison diary; her personal account of the trials, experiences, and visions in prison.
Sections 11–13	Saturus' description of his vision.
Sections 14–21	Redactor's conclusion; eyewitness narration of the actual martyrdom.

15. For an analysis of the authorship of the various sections, cf. Dodds, pp. 49–52; E. C. Owen, *Some Authentic Acts of the Early Martyrs* (Oxford: Clarendon, 1927), pp. 74–77; J. Armitage Robinson, *Texts and Studies* No. 2 (Cambridge: The University Press, 1891), I, 43–58; W. H. Shewring, *The Passion of Saints Perpetua and Felicity* (London: Sheed and Ward, 1931), pp. xviii–xxiii. For a general analysis and a translation of the account see Rosemary Rader, "*The Martyrdom of Perpetua:* A Protest Account of Third-Century Christianity," in Patricia Wilson-Kastner, *et al., A Lost Tradition: Women Writers of the Early Church* (Washington, D.C.: University Press of America, 1981), pp. 1–32.

While awaiting death, Perpetua was visited periodically by her pagan father and her Christian relatives and friends. All of them attempted without success to have her recant for the sake of her aged father and young child whom she was still nursing. Convinced by her brother that she was in a position to ask God for a vision of her future, Perpetua did so and learned through four subsequent visions that: she was not to be freed but was to prepare for martyrdom; her brother who had died some years previously was suffering and needed her help; her prayers and suffering would release her brother from his affliction; her victory as a martyr was assured (111–19). The redactor's conclusion graphically portrays the actual events of the martyrs' deaths just as Perpetua had prophesied (123–31).

Though Perpetua is the chief protagonist within the account, she acted as representative of both the male and female members united in a common effort to live by the dictates of conscience. Hence she reminded her father that just as all things had their proper name according to their essence, "so I also cannot be called anything else than what I am, a Christian" (109). She and her companions proclaimed their identity publicly in the Forum before the governor who condemned them to death for this conviction (113, 115).

The document provides invaluable testimony about the early Christian community of Carthage at the beginning of the third century, indicating principles which were to be permanent in the African church. Since the martyrs were recently converted, their beliefs and hopes as reflected in their visions reflect current catechetical teaching and provide insights into the eschatological beliefs of the Christian community. Perpetua, for example, confides that from the moment she entered prison, she felt the influence and direction of the Spirit who indicated to her that she was to request nothing but perseverance in her suffering (109). Three of the recorded visions predict the imminence and final victory of the ensuing tortures and death, but in each instance victory in resurrected life is the focus of the scenes.[16] The sense of equality which allowed the development of re-

---

16. *Acts,* pp. 11 and 117–23. Herbert Musurillo, *Symbolism and the Christian Imagination* (Baltimore: Helicon, 1962), p. 48, concludes that the document's major import lay in the fact that it was both an account of the actual sufferings of the martyrs and an apocalypse in its own right. He claims that its uniqueness "comes from the many visions the martyrs enjoyed before their death, told apparently in their own

ciprocal affections and mutual support among the martyrs-to-be was in part validated by the common belief in resurrection-fellowship.

The conviction of the imminence of the end of time encouraged and even demanded of the martyrs the rejection of their natural family and society. That these rejections were made not for any lack of sensitivity or disregard for the people involved is substantiated by Perpetua's narration of the anxiety experienced in realizing that she was the direct cause of her family's sufferings. In spite of her father's entreaties to recant, Perpetua remained firmly convinced that her rejections were justified and even demanded by an appeal to a duty greater than that expected of her as daughter. She reminded her father that God's will and power would prevail in that "we are not left to ourselves but are all in his [God's] power" (113). In their final meeting her father began to tear out his hair, fell on his face before his daughter, cursed his old age, and repeated utterances which moved everyone but his martyr-daughter (117).[17]

Perpetua had ultimately to reject even her child who transformed the prison existence for the short time that he was with her. Several days before her martyrdom, the infant was given to her father who refused to return him to Perpetua. She accepted this event as an act of a provident God, for "as God willed, the baby had no further desire for the breast, nor did I suffer any inflammation; and so I was relieved of any anxiety for my child and of any discomfort in my breasts" (115). The loss of her child effected a liberation toward a higher goal, a liberation symbolized by the harmonious concurrence of Perpetua's peace of mind with health of body.

One senses throughout the narrative the martyrs' attitude of defiance and rebellion against authority. In this account as in others, the powers of evil were personified in anyone attempting to dissuade the martyrs from loyalty to their faith. Even Perpetua's father whom she claimed to love dearly was severely judged because of his failure to understand her position. After one of several fierce disagreements

---

words." For an interesting Jungian analysis of Perpetua's visions, see Marie-Louise von Franz, "Die Passio Perpetuae," in C. G. Jung's *Aion* (Zurich: Roscher, 1951), pp. 389–496.

17. Cf. p. 29 where the belief in God's providence likewise allowed Agathonice to respond to the mob's request that she have pity on her son: "He has God who can take pity on him; for he has providence over all."

with him, she related how her father departed, "vanquished along with his diabolical arguments. For a few days afterwards I gave thanks to the Lord that I was separated from my father and I was comforted by his absence" (109).

The powers of evil were particularly personified in the Roman rulers and officials. The specific form of non-violent protest exhibited in the accounts is usually directed against the state officials responsible for the maintenance of peace and order in a certain province or city. For the Christian martyrs, justification for disobedience to civil authorities was derived from the theory that laws could and ought to be defied for the sake of moral principles, with final appeal being made to God as the highest authority. Hence, protest was an integral part of the revolutionary dynamic of martyrdom, especially when viewed in the light of the apocalyptic and prophetic nature of the martyrs' faith which justified martyrdom as a catalyst for transforming a death-process to a life-bearing one.

It is particularly in the depictions of the martyrs' fearless and sometimes hostile confrontations with the authorities that Perpetua emerged as spokesperson and initiator of action. She exhibited a fearless defiance, for example, as she protested the prisoners' maltreatment by the jailers. She reminded one of the jailers that the prisoners deserved better food and quarters since anyone appearing publicly in the arena on the emperor's birthday (the day of their martyrdom) ought to be in good condition. The jailer, apparently unaccustomed to such boldness on the part of a woman, trembled, blushed, and gave orders that the prisoners be treated more humanely (125). On the day of martyrdom Perpetua was ordered to wear the women prisoners' customary dress of the priestess of Ceres. She argued effectively that if the prisoners were interested in conforming to such regulations they would undoubtedly not be in prison; and since they had devoted their lives to the cause of freedom, they could not possibly acquiesce in such a request during these last moments of life (127).

The prisoners' view of martyrdom as ultimate victory allowed them to accept non-violence as a means of revenge against their persecutors. They need not take up arms against them since martyrdom itself was assurance of revenge hereafter when the positions of judge and judged would be reversed. This conviction is expressed by the

martyrs on the day of their death. As they marched past the proconsul in charge their motions and gestures indicated, "You have condemned us, but God will condemn you," actions causing the martyrs
the added inconvenience of being publicly scourged. Undaunted in
their loyalty, however, "they rejoiced at this that they had obtained a
share in the Lord's suffering" (127).

The martyrs' apparent impudence and boldness in speech must
be understood within the context of "free speech" as defined and em-
ployed by the cultures of that period. An essential sign of Greek
(and, later, Roman) democracy was the privilege of citizens to engage in free speech, to say anything publicly without fear of incrimi-
nation. This practice of candor in speech was likewise extended to
the private sphere whereby friends and family members enjoyed
varying degrees of *parrhesia,* freedom of speech.[18] When various phi-
losophies of the Hellenistic period adopted the concept its content
became primarily moral, i.e., the person of moral rectitude was allowed almost unrestrained speech. In this context *parrhesia* was often considered necessary in that it served truth. Hence, in the
Hebrew and New Testament scriptures the righteous enjoy *parrhesia,*
or access to God through communication; they can pray to him and
have their prayers heard.[19]

The public inquiries prior to martyrdom allowed the confessing
Christian a special opportunity to exhibit *parrhesia.* The fearlessness
of the martyrs' speech and actions stemmed from their conviction
that truth would ultimately conquer and would hasten their face-to-
face vision of God with whom they enjoyed a special kind of *parrhesia.*[20] The community's special claim to intimacy with God not only

---

18. For a general description of *parrhesia* in the Greek and Hellenistic world, see
M. Radin, "Freedom of Speech in Ancient Athens," *The American Journal of Philology,* 48 (1927), 215–20. For a study of the changes in meaning of *parrhesia* from early
Greek literature to the Christian martyr accounts see "Parrhesia," *Theological Dictionary of the New Testament,* V, 871–86, and Erik Peterson, "Zur Bedeutungsgeschichte
von Parrhesia," *Festschrift fur Reinhold Seeberg* (Leipzig, 1929), 283–97.

19. E.g., Job 27:10; Jn. 7:13, 10:24, 11:14; 2 Cor. 3:12; Heb. 10:35. Cf. the Perpetua account wherein she is urged to ask God for a prediction of her future. She agreed to
do so, "for I knew that I could speak with the Lord, whose great blessings I had come
to experience" (111). Paul Jouon discusses the various meanings of *parrhesia* in
"Divers Sens de Parrhesia dans le Nouveau Testament," *Recherches de Science Reli-
gieuse,* 30 (April 1940), 239–42.

20. In Eusebius, *Hist. Eccl.* V.1.49 and Origen, *Contra Cels.* II.45, *parrhesia* is

added greater group solidarity through the notion of spiritual equality, but served as edification to many who witnessed their fearlessness before judges and jailers.

The martyrs' unique relationship with God set them above and outside the normative ecclesial structures. Throughout the accounts, for example, the martyrs demonstrate their belief in the individual's ability to be the instrument of salvation with only the help of God and no other human intercessor, the individual's importance and worth being derived from merit rather than position. In Saturus' vision, for example, Perpetua was invoked by a bishop and a priest to reconcile the differences between them. Although she acknowledged their superiority within the ecclesiastical hierarchy, she saw them standing outside the gates of heaven, clearly separated from the martyrs within. Their function was chiefly disciplinary since the bishop is chided by the angels to correct his people "who approach you as though they had come from the games, quarreling about the different teams" (123). Perpetua as a martyr was the sole instrument of her salvation, a belief symbolized in the vision where the narrow ladder allowed the ascent of only one at a time (111, 113). She need not rely on a priest's mediation as she proceeded to reconcile herself with God and society; she could ask for visions on her own merit (113); she had the necessary intercessory power to release her brother from his suffering (115, 117); as a laywoman she interceded for a bishop and a priest (121, 123); and since the account intimated that martyrdom was a second baptism assuring salvation without priestly mediation, she could effect her salvation by direct combat with the powers of evil (127, 129, 131).

The overall picture presented by the account is that of a group of Carthaginians subscribing to a new religion which allowed for membership in a more egalitarian society than that allowed by their contemporary standards. Though a major portion of the account contains repeated references to concerns generally identified as fe-

---

viewed as a special charism of the early martyrs. This unique perogative derived from their friendship with the Lord through imitation of his death. D. Smolders, in "L'audace de l'apotre selon St. Paul, le theme de la parresia," *Collectanea Mechliniensa* (Louvain, 1958), 16–30 and 117–33, asserts that *parrhesia* must have been current in the primitive community, especially in relation with persecutions where the term expressed both audacity before men and assurance before God.

male in nature (e.g., child-bearing, nursing, filial regard for father, sisterly concern for brother, maternal solicitude for infant), to concentrate on these elements is to distort the image which Perpetua, Saturus, and the redactor present. The martyrs' conscious awareness of being first and foremost "Christian," and with God's help "martyr," allowed little concern for traditional sex-role differentiation. Although Perpetua, for example, is the chief character in the events depicted, her actions are never detrimental to or pejorative of the male members of the group.[21]

The image which emerges of Perpetua is that of the Christian female *and* male, the "every-person" of the early Christian Church in North Africa who aspired toward positive assurance of salvation. Perpetua is described, for example, in feminine terms as she walked from the prison to the arena on the day of martyrdom "as the beloved of God, as a wife of Christ." But her countenance exhibited boldness and directness as she put down everyone's stare by her own piercing gaze (127). What is intimated here is best expressed by Perpetua herself as she recounted her last vision. She indicated that as she was about to battle with the Egyptian, "My clothes were stripped off, and suddenly I was a man. My seconds began to rub me down with oil (as they are wont to do before a contest)" (119). In keeping with the spirit of the narration it seems consistent to interpret this as symbolic of the necessity to prove oneself in battle before attaining the final prize. Since women were ordinarily not combatants in public games, both Perpetua's modesty and the metaphor's intent suffered less by her male appearance. The trainer was apparently not deceived, for immediately after the battle he kissed her, handed her the branch of victory and said, "Peace be with you, my daughter" (119). The section is an appropriate climax to the scene in that Perpetua appeared as both female and male, an intimation that spiritual equality validated the interchange of sexual imagery without loss of essential meaning.

Perpetua's last recorded acts on earth exemplified her courage and successful protest against what was possibly a culturally accepted sexist bias. Perpetua was to be killed in the arena by a mad cow se-

---

21. Although Saturus plays an important role as instructor of the group, it is Perpetua who is the forceful leader, even in Saturus' vision (119–23).

lected so that the women's sex "might be matched with that of the beast" (129). She survived the attack and was hence to be executed by the sword. Anticipating the beginning of the heavenly life which she had foreseen in her visions, Perpetua willingly participated in the completion of her martyrdom. When the novice swordsman struck the knife into her bone, Perpetua took his trembling hand and guided it to her throat. The redactor adds the eulogistic note: "It was as though so great a woman, feared as she was by the unclean spirit, could not be dispatched unless she herself were willing" (130). Thus the redactor completed the image of Perpetua as leader of a prison community whose recorded actions and sayings projected the belief in equality of persons. Lefkowitz observes:

> It is not without significance that the religion which Perpetua adopts appears to encourage more a-sexual, fraternal relationships between men and women, and that the men with whom she dies and whom she sees in her visions are benign, supportive, and beautiful. . . . [22]

Undoubtedly the prospect of dying together was a major factor in creating the type of benign and supportive egalitarian community described in this and other accounts. But the fact that the martyrs' world provided the ideals inspiring a choice of death rather than denial of those ideals indicates the importance ascribed to them. The loving relationships portrayed between slave and master, neophyte and instructor, male and female, speak eloquently of the lack of concern for social, racial, or sexual distinctions.

In both the recounting of actual events and explanations of the visions of Perpetua and Saturus, there are indications of Perpetua's close personal friendship particularly with Saturus, Pomponius (a certain deacon), and Felicitas. It was Saturus who appeared in Perpetua's first vision as guide and helper as she and he attempted to climb the celestial ladder guarded by the devil in the form of a dragon (111). Likewise, in Saturus' first vision Perpetua was the first to whom he spoke as he arrived in Heaven: "And I said to Perpetua

---

22. Mary R. Lefkowitz, "The Motivation for St. Perpetua's Martyrdom," *Journal of the American Academy of Religion,* 44 (September 1976), 417–21.

(for she was at my side): 'This is what the Lord promised us. We
have received his promise' " (119, 121). Pomponius, for some reason
not imprisoned as a Christian, daily visited the martyrs, took care of
their needs, intervened for Perpetua to her father, and appeared in
Perpetua's last vision as the agent responsible for her release from
prison (109, 115, 118). It was for love of Felicitas that Perpetua for-
got her own pain and injuries after she had been mauled by the mad
cow in the arena. According to the redactor, Perpetua arose: "And
seeing that Felicitas had been crushed to the ground, she went over
to her, gave her her hand, and lifted her up. Then the two stood side
by side" (129).

Perpetua, like the rest of the martyrs, was never alone in any of
her struggles. Both the kiss of peace and the mutual sharing of the
agape or love feast served to sustain the martyrs' courage. As they
were about to be killed by the sword,

> . . . the mob asked that their bodies be brought out into the
> open that their eyes might be the guilty witnesses of the
> sword that pierced their flesh. And so the martyrs got up
> and went to the spot of their own accord as the people
> wanted them to, and kissing one another they sealed their
> martyrdom with the ritual kiss of peace (131).

Both the redactor's introduction and conclusion to the account
speak of the events' importance as recent and valid signs of "new
prophecies" and "new vision" (107, 131). He indicates that he himself had been duly inspired to write of the events "so that those of
you that were witnesses may recall the glory of the Lord and those
that now learn of it through hearing may have fellowship with the
holy martyrs and, through them, with the Lord Christ Jesus" (107,
109). That the "new vision" and "fellowship with . . . the Lord
Christ Jesus" allowed for more personal friendships between men
and women is attested even more forcefully by the literature of a subsequent age which practiced a spiritual symbolic martyrdom of asceticism.

The maintenance of the egalitarianism demonstrated by the
martyr communities was effected chiefly by the martyrs' personal
identification with Christ as martyr/exemplar, and by solidarity

among the members as brothers and sisters in Christ.[23] In the world created within the fairly short-lived prison communities, the martyrs' anticipation of a life of immortality placed them in a position of liminality, i.e., they were neither of this world nor yet caught up in the next. As such the members were akin to what Turner describes as "liminal *personae*" or "threshold people" whose way of life was characterized by an intense comradeship and egalitarianism undercutting secular distinctions of rank and status.[24]

In the unstructured and undifferentiated existence of the martyrs' liminal state, the only valid authority recognized by them was that of Christ and of those martyrs-designate whose actions betrayed the closest approximation to the Christ/exemplar. That the martyrs' example spoke powerfully to future generations of Christians is witnessed by the rapid spread within the Church of the cult of the martyrs. From the middle of the third century the private commemoration of the martyrs' birth dates in heaven began to pass into the official and public liturgy of the Church.

When, however, the literal imitation of the martyrs was no longer so easily accessible, the martyrs' death was symbolically relived as an internalized dying daily to self. This spiritual death and rebirth was best exemplified by the celibate monastic whose way of life was similar to that of the martyr's in purpose and motivation, but different in mode of attainment. But even before monasticism was institutionalized into the early Christian structures another phenomenon was occurring which heralded a distinct paradigm shift in male/female relationships. That unique Christian phenomenon was *syneisaktism,* "spiritual marriage" between a man and a woman whose mutuality of goals allowed a life-style rarely experienced outside the early Christian communities.

---

23. That the early Christians demonstrated this solidarity is attested by both Christian and non-Christian writers. Cf. Tertullian, *Apol.* 39.7 and 50.14; Minucius Felix, *Octav.* 37; *Apology of Aristides 13; Justin, I Apol.* 14 and 37.

24. Victor W. Turner, *The Ritual Process: Structure and Anti-Structure* (Chicago: Aldine, 1969), p. 95. Though Turner's study deals chiefly with initiation rites, Chapter Three, "Liminality and Communitas," pp. 94–130, presents material from which interesting parallels can be drawn for the martyrdom process which because of its "betwixt and between" nature was a type of liminal position.

CHAPTER FIVE

Syneisaktism: Spiritual Marriage

In the late fourth century C.E. Jerome, in a letter to Eustochium, one of his closest friends among the noble women of Rome, asked how the "plague" of the *agapetae* came to exist within the Church. He calls these *agapetae* "unwedded wives," "novel concubines, and harlots."

> I call them such even though they cling to one partner. They share the same house, the same room, and often the same bed, and yet they call us suspicious if we think anything amiss. A brother leaves his unmarried sister; a virgin, slighting her unmarried brother, seeks a brother in a stranger. Both profess one purpose, to derive spiritual consolation from those not related to them.[1]

The *agapetae* mentioned by Jerome were women who lived with laymen or unmarried clergy as sisters in a kind of spiritual marriage called *syneisaktism.*[2] From the scant references to the phenomenon we can surmise that celibate men and women vowed their lives to

---

1. *Ep.* 22, PL 22:402–3. Unless otherwise indicated, the translations are my own. Much of the material for this chapter was presented at the Institute on the Origins of Monastic Spirituality, June 1980, at St. John's University, Collegeville, Minnesota, and published in *The Continuing Quest for God: Monastic Spirituality in Tradition and Transition* (Collegeville, Minnesota: The Liturgical Press, 1982), pp. 80–87.

2. In the East these women were called "agapetae" or "gyne syneisaktos"; in the West, "agapetae," "virgines subintroductae," "mulieres adoptivae," or "mulieres extraneae." The only general study of the phenomenon is by Hans Achelis, *Virgines*

God and lived together for mutual support and encouragement. It may be such *agapetae* to which Paul refers when he demands of some critics, "have we not every right ... to take a Christian woman round with us, like all the other apostles and brothers of the Lord and Cephas?"[3] Although "woman" may also be translated "wife," there is no strong evidence to discount the possibility of her being a celibate choosing to minister to the needs of the missionary group in the same way that Priscilla and Phoebe, for example, shared in such ministry.[4]

Exactly how the practice originated is not clear, but the repeated admonitions against it by various patristic writers, and the long line of synodal injunctions and canons prohibiting its continuance, intimates its existence within Christian communities of both East and West in the first five or six centuries. One can conjecture, however, that certain Christians chose a type of spiritual relationship in which a male and a female celibate lived together as brother and sister for mutual support and edification.

The custom of the time demanded that an unmarried or widowed woman be under the tutelage of a male relative, and for lack of a relative a guardian or *patronus* would be appointed to assure the woman's personal and legal protection.[5] Hence Jerome objected to the custom of the *agapetae* who were bypassing the prescribed guardianship by association with a non-related male. The practice may

---

Subintroductae (Leipzig: J. D. Hinrich, 1902). Cf. P. de Labriolle, "Le Mariage spirituel dans l'Antiquite chretienne," *Revue Historique,* 136 (1921), 204–25; and Henry C. Lea, *History of Sacerdotal Celibacy in the Christian Church,* 2 vols. (London: Williams and Norgate, 1907), pp. 43–49. The former argues that *syneisaktism* was practiced only in heretical groups, but the fact that letters and decrees refer to specific persons and groups practicing it in the Christian communities contradicts that view. Cf. 1 Cor. 7:36–38 where Paul advises either the husband or fiancé of a *parthenos* (usually translated "young, unmarried woman") that though it is all right to marry the girl, still it is better to allow her to remain a virgin. Some exegetes consider the passage a case of a father or guardian giving the girl in marriage, but most agree that the general usage of the word *parthenos* suggests its reference to a woman who agreed to set up house with a man in order to be an economically independent ascetic.

   3. 1 Cor. 9:5.
   4. Acts 18:18; Rom. 16:1–12; 2 Tim. 4:19.
   5. In the Roman world, male guardianship over females was theoretically in force until the time of Diocletian (ruled C.E. 285–305), though the practice continued for several centuries. See Sarah B. Pomeroy, *Goddesses, Whores, Wives, and Slaves: Women in Classical Antiquity* (New York: Schocken Books, 1975), pp. 149–89.

have been tolerated because of the early Christians' notion of the Christian community as *familia,* a household of those professing belief in the teachings of Christ. Therefore a spiritual relationship between a "brother" and "sister" in Christ may have been the Christians' earliest response to ascetic aspirations.

This type of spiritual marriage built upon a shared pursuit of perfection had some precedent among the Neoplatonists who, like the Pythagoreans and Epicureans, welcomed membership by women interested in the pursuit of philosophy. Porphyry, for example, in 302 C.E., already advanced in age, married Marcella, the widow of a philosopher friend. In a letter to Marcella he declared that he married her because she and her former husband had shared in his philosophic endeavors, and he desired to become the support she had lost by leading her to those heights for which he himself yearned.[6] According to Geffcken, Porphyry's true asceticism appears not in his treatise, *On Abstinence from Animal Food,* but in this letter "which begins with his motives for entering into this marriage, namely to draw the woman of his choice into the complete selflessness which he professed himself."[7]

But as important as celibacy may have been for the attainment of wisdom and the good life of the non-Christian philosophers, nowhere is celibacy allotted such importance as in Christian writings of the third and fourth centuries C.E. Even in early popular belief there was the conviction that asexuality was necessary for the millennium.[8] The plan for perfect Christian living, therefore, was based on a denial of sexuality which would return human nature to its prelapsarian state. Hence Ambrose could write, "In saintly virgins we see on earth the life of the angels we lost in paradise."[9] The continent or

6. *Ad Marcellam,* in *Porphyrii Philosophi Platonici Opuscula Selecta,* ed. Augustus Nauck (Leipzig: Teubner, 1963), pp. 273–75. For an English translation see, *Porphyry the Philosopher to His Wife Marcella,* trans. Alice Zimmern (London: George Redway, 1896), pp. 54–55.

7. Johannes Geffcken, *The Last Days of Greco-Roman Paganism,* trans. Sabine MacCormack (New York: North Holland Publishing Company, 1978), p. 71.

8. Cf. The "Acts" of John, Peter, Andrew, Thomas in *New Testament Apocrypha,* Vol. II, ed. Edgar Hennecke and William Schneemelcher, trans. R. McWilson (Philadelphia: Westminster, 1963), pp. 188–259, 275, 390–531. The view expressed is that sexual purity is a prerequisite of salvation.

9. *De. Inst. Virg.* 104 (PL 16:345). Cf. Gregory of Nyssa, *De Hom. Opif.* 17 (PG 44:188–89), *De Virg.* 2 (PG 46:324), Methodius, *Symposium* 2.7, trans. and annot.

asexual life was considered an "angelic" one (*Vita Angelica*) in that by not marrying, individuals "are equal to the angels, and are children of God, being children of the resurrection."[10] Hence, the practice of *syneisaktism* may be attributed to the notion in early Christian societies that a man and woman aspiring toward the most perfect way of life could live together as celibates in a shared *vita angelica.*

This way of life cannot be accurately assessed except within the early Christian context of grace. Hans Achelis points out that the early Christians had such absolute confidence in divine grace operative within them that all things, even the "unnatural," were possible.[11] Hence what may have seemed strange or impossible to another culture or another moment in time was considered one of many instances of divine power at work in the world.

Another factor which undoubtedly enabled *syneisaktism* to occur was millenarianism, i.e., the early Christian groups' belief that the second coming of Christ was imminent. Hence, the normative life, marriage, was no longer considered essential or even necessary for society. In such societies where the basic concern was preparation for the end of time, celibacy loomed large as the means toward the attainment of a personal state of perfection. And in an age when monastic communities were not yet as organized or accessible as they were later to become, the phenomenon of *syneisaktism* emerged as a practical way of life for those choosing celibacy. In such an arrangement not only did the partners mutually encourage and exhort each other to persevere in the pursuit of perfection, but there was also the practical consequence of male protection for the young woman.

Although there is little or no mention of the names of individuals living in this manner, there is sufficient evidence that the practice survived in various regions as late as the seventh century. During this century ecclesiastics at the Council of Bordeaux were still forbidding the practice which had been outlawed by at least ten previous councils and synods since the third century. The little evidence there is about the phenomenon is derived chiefly from third and fourth

---

Herbert Musurillo (Westminster, Maryland: Newman Press, 1958), p. 57.

10. Lk. 20:35–36. Cf. Mt. 21:30 and Mk. 12:25. For a detailed study of the *vita angelica* concept in early monasticism see Jean Leclerq, *The Life of Perfection,* trans. Leonard J. Doyle (Collegeville, Minnesota: Liturgical Press, 1961), pp. 15–42.

11. *Op. cit.,* p. 74.

century injunctions against the practice.

Eusebius narrated how Paul of Samosata, bishop of Antioch, was condemned by the Council of Antioch in 206 because, along with other questionable practices, he was living with some "adopted sisters as the inhabitants of Antioch call them."[12] Although there was no proof that the relationship was anything but "spiritual," he was chided for the potential scandal evoked by such a practice.[13]

A half century later Cyprian of Carthage was asked by a priest, Pomponius, about the proper procedure for dealing with virgins who vowed celibacy but had chosen to live with men in a chaste relationship. Cyprian advised:

> We must interfere at once with such as these, that they may be separated while yet they can be separated in innocence; because by and by they will not be able to be separated by our interference, after they have become joined together by a very guilty conscience. Moreover, what a number of serious mischiefs we see to have arisen hence; and what a multitude of virgins we behold corrupted by unlawful and dangerous conjunctions of this kind, to our great grief of mind.[14]

Cyprian thus indicates that the practice was no longer deemed acceptable in North Africa by the middle of the third century. It is difficult to ascertain whether the practice had become justifiably reprehensible or whether the bishops felt that their authority as "fathers" of the extended Christian family was being usurped by the male partners in the "spiritual marriage." By the fourth century especially, a fairly sophisticated hierarchical structure had been developed by the Christian leaders, and the *episcopus* was deemed the overseer of the Church's morality, hierarchy, and revenues. The laymen and unmarried clergy who had *agapetae* were thus viewed as usurpers of the power of the local episcopal *patronus,* and hence the injuction against the practice.

---

12. *Hist. Eccl.* 7.30, PG 20:716.

13. *Idem.*

14. *Ep.* 61. *Anti-Nicene Christian Library,* trans. R. E. Wallis, 8 (Edinburgh: T. and T. Clark, 1868), p. 205. Cf. Pseudo-Cyprian, *Ep.* 4; *De Sing. Cler.*

John Chrysostom, in two separate treatises, provided the lengthiest invectives against the practice: one inveighed against those men who lived with "virgin partners" (*parthenos syneisaktos*), the other against women who had vowed celibacy but were residing with men. Chrysostom noted that the practice was a fairly recent and unusual one; that its adherents gave a number of reasons for its existence (none of which Chrysostom accepted); that although it was intended for mutual exhortation and considered by the participants as a pleasant and joy-filled relationship, it was in reality a "playing with fire"; that both Christ and Paul warned of the punishments accruing to those who gave scandal of this nature; that the practice was an attempt to serve both God and mammon; that the rewards of living alone as a celibate far outweighed the risks encountered when male and female celibates lived together.[15] According to Palladius, one of the reasons for Chrysostom's exile from the patriarchate of Constantinople in C.E. 404 was the result of the clergy's anger at his serious attempts to eradicate this practice.[16] Chrysostom's treatises, like the bulk of literature either questioning or condemning the practice, indicate that the participants' motives may have been commendable and the cohabitation celibate, but the danger of possible scandal to the surrounding community and the threat to the preservation of the participants' celibacy demanded the discontinuance of the practice.[17]

The fear of scandal was generally the reason stated for the reprimands and the prohibitions of the practice. The local synods of Elvira (about 306)[18] and Ancyra (314)[19] had already prohibited the practice, and the first general or ecumenical council, Nicea (325), stated: "The great Synod has stringently forbidden any bishop, pres-

---

15. PG 47:495–532. For an English translation of and an introduction to the two essays see Elizabeth A. Clark, *Jerome, Chrysostom, and Friends: Essays and Translations* (New York: Edwin Mellen Press, 1979), pp. 158–248.

16. *Dial. Hist. Pall.,* PG 47:20.

17. Cf. Pseudo-Cyprian, *De Sing. Cler.*; Jerome, *Ep.* 22.117 and 128, and *The Life of Malchus;* Epiphanius, *Panar. Haeres.* 63; Caesarius of Arles, *Sermon* 41; and Gregory the Great, *Ep.* 9:60 and 106; 10.23. Other specific examples of early prohibitions against *syneisaktism* are included in the Iro-Italian Collection in *Vat. Lat.* 1339, fol. 72v–76v; *Vat. Lat.* 6093, fol. 127v–29v.

18. Can. 27. Sources for the study of the canons are: PL 84 and Karl Joseph Hefele, *Histoire des Conciles d'apres les Documents originaux,* trans. and rev. by Henri Leclerq, 11 vols. (Paris: Letouzey et Ane, 1907–52); NPNF, Ser. 2.14.

19. Can. 19.

byter, deacon, or any of the clergy whatever, to have a *subintroducta* dwelling with him, except only a mother, or sister, or aunt, or such persons only as are beyond suspicion."[20] The message was reiterated almost word for word in some instances in later synods and councils. An edict of Honorius and Theodosius II (420) was supportive of the Church's efforts to eradicate it by legal pronouncement.

> For it follows good morals that clergymen serving the sacred ministries should not be joined to extraneous women, whom they excuse by the stained association of the appellation of "sister".... But although it [depravity] does not penetrate into this association and friendship, rumor contaminates and the addition of the other sex affords occasion for evil morals.... Since these things are so [you] should publish by edicts posted everywhere ... that whoever are supported by the priesthood of any rank whatever or are distinguished by the honour of the clericate should realize that association with extraneous women are prohibited to them, with only this faculty conceded to them: that they keep within the precincts of their homes mothers, daughters, and blood sisters, for in respect to these the natural bond permits no perverse crime to be considered.[21]

The repetition of such injunctions may have been due to a variety of reasons. Certain patristic writers, Cyprian and John Chrysostom, for example, may have been so blinded by their own prudery as to imagine or elaborate certain incidents, thus confusing fact and fiction. Others, like Jerome, prone to the exaggerations often effected by a full-blown rhetorical style, caused the kernel of fact (when such was present) to be blown completely out of proportion. Also, the compilers of edicts and decrees may simply have incorporated *in toto* certain portions of past decrees without proof of their necessity. This

---

20. Can. 3, NPNF, Ser. 2.14, p. 11. Cf. Arabic Canon IV, attributed to the Council of Nicea, p. 46.

21. *C.S.* 10, in P.R. Coleman–Norton, *Roman State and Christian Church: A collection of Legal Documents to A.D. 503* (London: SPCK, 1966), II.612–13. Cf. *C.T.* 9.25.3; 16.2.44; *C.I.* 1.3.19. The mention of daughters being allowed to live in the cleric's home indicates the non-celibate nature of the cleric's relationship with a "spiritual sister," or indicates that the cleric was married before becoming a priest.

is not to deny, however, that certain isolated incidents of non-compliance to previous injunctions did occur. Basil, for example, threatened a certain seventy-year-old priest with the choice of excommunication or separation from a woman residing with him. Citing Canon 3 of the Council of Nicea, Basil suggested that the priest send the woman to live with a group of celibate women.[22] Gregory the great, ordering the bishops of France to summon a synod for the correction of certain abuses, repeated the previous injunctions but added a consolatory note.

> For of what profit is it to have guarded all besides this—if through one place pernicious access be afforded to the enemy? Therefore let women be prohibited from living with those who are constituted in any sacred order. With regard to them . . . it must be laid down by the consent of all that they may have no other women with them but those whom the sacred canons include. And though this interdiction is perhaps bitter for the time to come, there is no doubt that it will afterwards grow sweet from its very benefit to their souls, if the enemy be overcome in that whereby he might have overcome them.[23]

Most of the later councils do not directly stress the condemnation of the practice but instead legislate against clerics' association with all but a select group of women whose familial ties to the clerics presumably minimized the dangers to celibacy.[24] Reynolds maintains that the practice lingered for a longer period than most scholars admit, and he attempts to demonstrate that "the practice existed far into the Middle Ages particularly in Celtic and then in Anglo-Saxon milieus and that, far from being a Celtic skeleton-in-the-closet, Celtic *syneisaktism* represented one of the most primitive aspects of Christianity to survive in medieval Western Europe."[25]

22. Can. 89, NPNF, Ser. 2.14, p. 610.

23. *Ep.* 9.106, NPNF, Ser. 2.13, p. 26.

24. E.g., Council of Telensis (386), Can. 9; Geronda (517), Can. 7; 5th Council of Orleans (549), Can. 3; Braga (561), Can. 32; Tours (567), Can. 11; Macon (583), Can.1; Toledo (589), Can. 5; Hispalis (590), Can. 3; 4th Council of Toledo (633), Can. 42–43; Bordeaux (663–75), Can. 3; and 3rd Council of Nice (787), Can. 8.

25. Roger E. Reynolds, *"Virgines Subintroductae* in Celtic Christianity," *Har-*

Although there is no direct evidence that the practice allowed women many social advantages, the fact remains that for some time within early Christian history, particularly within the first few centuries which were generally considered its charismatic phase, men and women felt free to communicate and establish mutual relationships on a very personal and intimate level. The practice of *syneisaktism* or celibate cohabitation was an external expression of the Christians' belief in a new age which allowed an expansion of the normative male/female husband/wife relationship. While under the protection of a male celibate partner the female celibate was accorded a freedom, a dignity, and an importance not granted to her married woman-counterpart.

It is uncertain whether the practice was chiefly espoused by groups like the Montanists and Gnostics who generally allowed a greater degree of mobility to the women within the sects.[26] A correlation is suggested by the fact that the practice was being prohibited and occurred less frequently after the third and fourth centuries, at which time the more liberal Christian sects were already separating themselves from other Christian groups or were being expelled as heretical. For a variety of reasons (e.g., actual abuses, fear of scandal, jealousy of prelates) *syneisaktism* gradually disappeared, but a new ideal developed which allowed the continuance of celibate relationships between male and female celibates.[27] Though the degree of intimacy may have diminished, the need for encouragement in aspiring

---

vard Theological Review, 61 (October 1968), 548, refutes the argument of Nora Chadwick, *The Age of Saints in the Early Celtic Church* (London: Oxford University Press, 1961), p. 149, where she claims that many of the extreme provisions in the Irish penitentials, among which are those against *virgines subintroductae,* are due to the Irish love of casuistry, hypothetical legal analysis, and theoretical cases. Reynolds argues, as I do, that the repetition of texts and later injunctions against *syneisaktism* are proof of the practice's actual occurrence.

26. This aspect is further discussed by M. Zscharnack, *Der Dienst der Frau in den ersten Jahrhunderten der Christlichen Kirche* (Goettingen: Vendenhoeck, 1902), pp. 156ff. For an interpretative study of the characteristics of androgyny in certain Gnostic texts see Elaine H. Pagels, "The Gnostic Vision," *Parabola,* 3 (November 1978), 6–9.

27. Achelis, *op. cit.* p. 74, concludes his study of *syneisaktism* with the admission of his own amazement that this "geistige Ehe" endured as an ideal for at least two hundred years. He sees the phenomenon as something which should serve not as a source of embarrassment for Christianity, but as "ein Zeichen fur die Idealitat ihrer Jugendzeit."

toward mutual goals of perfection fostered a new ideal, the monastic or communal life.[28] And it is within the monastic structure that one finds more direct evidence of heterosexual friendship between specific individuals.

---

28. Though the origins of the double monasteries (communities of men and women within one area, both generally under the rule of one person, usually an abbess) is unclear, it seems plausible that they arose as a natural sequel to *syneisaktism,* especially in their earliest period of growth from the fourth to the eighth century. As the one-to-one relationship within *syneisaktism* was eliminated the double monastery may have developed out of practical necessity; men were needed by the women-monastics to carry on the ministerial functions and the more strenuous labor. For further studies on the origins of the double monasteries see Mary Bateson, "Origin and Early History of Double Monasteries," *Transactions of the Royal Historical Society,* 13 (1899), 139–98, and Alex H. Thompson, "Double Monasteries and the Male Element in Nunneries," in *The Ministry of Women* (London, 1919), Appendix VIII, pp. 145–64.

CHAPTER SIX

Celibacy and the Monastic Life

If the practice of *syneisaktism* created a climate conducive to a paradigm shift in male/female relationships, it was the monastic celibate life which ultimately established the new paradigm. Already during the gradual decline of the spiritually-oriented husband/wife phenomenon the monastic way of life was on the rise in Christian societies. Although the Christian ascetic ideal was present since Christianity's inception, it was during the fourth to the sixth centuries that it gained momentum. During this period many of the early Christian groups of ascetics (e.g., the Order of Widows, the Order of Virgins, groups of desert dwellers) passed through various stages of development to the more structured forms of monasticism (e.g., the regimented communes of Pachomius and the familially-ordered communities of Benedict). The growth of the Christian monastic movement ran parallel to the increasing importance allotted to celibacy as the most effective aid toward salvation.

When Constantine in the early fourth century allowed Christians the freedom to practice their religion, identification with Christ through martyrdom became less accessible except as the Christian's daily "dying to self" through asceticism became a symbolic reenactment of Christ's death. Just as Christians within the first three centuries considered martyrdom the most perfect imitation of Christ, so now a life of celibacy, progressively regarded as a major aspect of the self-discipline involved in dying daily, was viewed as a lifelong martyrdom.[1] Aiding the legitimation of celibacy was the abolition of so-

---

1. For a more detailed anlaysis of the martyr/monk correlation see William A. Clebsch, *Christianity in European History* (New York: Oxford, 1979), pp. 31–84, and Edward E. Malone, *The Monk and the Martyr* (Washington: Catholic University of America Press, 1950).

cial obstacles which Roman law had previously imposed on the unmarried and the childless. Many of these restrictions were abolished by Constantine who thus granted celibacy the aura of civil as well as ecclesiastical approbation.[2]

By the year 300 C.E. there were many ascetics leading a solitary life of symbolic martyrdom in Egypt, Syria, Palestine, Mesopotamia, and Persia.[3] Both men and women participated in the eremitic life as recluses on the outskirts of cities or in the desert, though the majority of female ascetics joined groups of women's celibate communities. Antony, for example, placed his sister with such a group when he decided to disburse his wealth and undertake the ascetic life.[4]

Both the *Apophthegmata* and the *Lausiac History* contain references to devout women living an ascetic life as strenuous as that of the men. Of the sixty-eight histories of hermits and monks recorded in the Syrian version of the *Lausiac History,* for example, nineteen are devoted to the lives of women ascetics whose spiritual prowess merited recognition. Although many of the women mentioned in these works lived in communities of celibate women (presumably for their own physical safety and the preservation of their virginity), there were numerous instances of women solitaries who confounded

---

2. Sozomen, *Hist. Eccl.* 1.9.

3. Primary sources of information about these desert dwellers are Palladius' *Lausiac History* and the *Apophthegmata Patrum (Sayings of the Fathers,* a collection of aphorisms, questions and answers of the more celebrated spiritual teachers). The source used for Palladius' *Lausiac History* is Anan-Isho's seventh century Syriac compilation, *The Paradise or Garden of the Holy Fathers,* Vol. I, trans. Ernest A. Wallis Budge (London: Chatto and Windus, 1907), hereafter cited as *Laus. Hist.* The source for the *Sayings* is *The Sayings of the Desert Fathers: The Alphabetical Collection,* trans. Benedicta Ward (London: A. R. Mowbray, 1975), hereafter cited as *Sayings.* One of the many problems with the text of the *Sayings* is that it appeared first in oral form and later in Coptic, Syriac, Greek, and Latin editions. Many changes had occurred in the process of retelling, rearranging and editing the materials. See Jean-Claude Guy, *Recherches sur la Tradition Greque des Apophthegmata Patrum* (Bruxelles: Societe des Bollandistes, 1962) and E. Schwartz, "Palladiana," *Zeitschrift fur die Neutestamentliche Wissenschaft und die Kunde der Alteren Kirche,* 36 (1937), 161–204. Useful secondary sources are *The Lausiac History of Palladius,* ed. Cuthbert Butler (Hildesheim: Georg Olms, 1967), pp. 173–297; Derwas J. Chitty, *The Desert A City: An Introduction to the Study of Egyptian and Palestian Monasticism under the Christian Empire* (Oxford: Basil Blackwell, 1966); and Arthur Vööbus, *A History of Asceticism in the Syrian Orient,* 184, 197, 239 (Louvain: Corpus Scriptorum Christianorum Orientalium, 1958–1963).

4. *Vita Ant.* 3.

and astonished others by their desert-heroics.[5] But the very nature of this solitary life allowed less opportunity for selective identification with others; hence there are fewer recorded instances of heterosexual friendship among the solitaries than among the ascetics within communities.

Several of the accounts, however, reflect the prevailing view that a life of celibacy was more salvific than marriage. In these instances husbands and wives mutually consented to dedicate themselves to a life of celibacy. Ammon, for example, having been forced by his uncle to marry, told his bride on the evening of their marriage, "Henceforth thou shalt be my lady and my sister; come therefore, and I will relate unto thee concerning a matter which is more excellent than marriage."[6] After reminding his bride of the corruptibility of earthly marriage he asked that they both retain their virginity in preparation for the incorruptible marriage feast in heaven. So they lived in the same house for eighteen years, meeting only for meals and daily prayer. When Ammon's wife decided that his spiritual excellence ought to be shared with more people, Ammon went to Mount Nitria where for twenty-two years he served as spiritual director to countless numbers of ascetics, visiting his wife twice a year.

The account of the Galatian couple, Heronian and Bosphoria, indicates the extent to which some felt compelled to answer the call to asceticism. Because of their confidence in the happiness of the afterlife, they organized their life around a monastic structure. They gave all their money to charitable institutions, lived chastely, dressed in modest and simple garb, and lessened the threat of failing in their intent by avoiding the company of other people. Their motives were clearly other-worldly because "with the eyes of the understanding they had already looked upon the good things which had been for ever prepared for them."[7]

The importance attributed to celibacy was likewise reflected in the recounting of the drastic punishments considered equitable for

---

5. E.g., Sara who chided her ascetic brothers with, "It is I who am a man, you who are women," *Sayings,* p. 193. Cf. *Sayings,* pp. 71–72 and 193–97, and *Laus. Hist.,* pp. 96, 140–42, 150–51, 173–201, 166, 240, 269. Considering the evidence, the title, *Sayings of the Fathers,* is not an accurate one since the texts contain sayings and deeds of both men and women.

6. *Laus. Hist.,* p. 100.

7. *Ibid.,* p. 167. Cf. Eucharistos and Mary, *Sayings,* p. 149.

those repudiating their promise of celibacy. There was a certain man in Scete, Stephana, who for twenty-nine years lived an exemplary celibate life and had even received the gift of healing. But the knowledge of his spiritual excellence produced in him an arrogance which soon led to his abandonment of the ascetic life. He subsequently lived very recklessly, going so far as to carry off a woman celibate so "that he might fulfill his wanton desire."[8] After two years of living together, thieves broke into his home, robbed him, bound the two of them and set fire to the house. Both died in the fire which was considered a sign of the eternal flames of hell which tormented the wicked.[9]

According to one account, death was considered preferable to the renunciation of one's promise to live celibately. A certain disciple of an older ascetic was so "attacked by the lust of fornication" that he left his cell, returned to the world, and decided to get married. Upon hearing the news the older ascetic was greatly disturbed and begged God to intervene. On the evening of the marriage the former ascetic died and was thus "not polluted with the union of marriage."[10]

Other accounts likewise demonstrate the increasing importance allotted to celibacy from the time of the "spiritual marriage" phenomenon (second through fourth century) to the proliferation of monastic communities (fourth through sixth century). The increasing emphasis on celibacy did in fact play a major role in the demise of the spiritual relationship in that the intimacy posed a potential threat to the celibacy of the individuals involved. Before analyzing the par-

---

8. *Ibid.*, p. 261.

9. *Ibid.*, p. 262.

10. *The Paradise or Garden of the Holy Fathers,* Vol. II, trans. Ernest A. Wallis Budge (London: Chatto and Windus, 1907), p. 217. Cf. p. 259. It is important to remember that the *Lausiac History* and *The Sayings,* compiled in the seventh century by Anon-Isho, are deeply Hellenistic and therefore greatly influenced by the Gnostic concept of body/soul dualism. Therefore, the selections chosen were frequently those which placed greater emphasis on the dichotomy between the material (body/evil) and the spiritual (soul/good). In spite of this, the general attitude on family life and legitimate conjugal relationships is one of respect and dignity. There is no wholesale disparagement of the marriage state or disdain for certain of its normal occupational hazards (e.g., pregnancy, birth, rearing of children), attitudes exhibited by other writers displaying harsher encratite tendencies. See the Pseudo-Clementine *Homily* and the apocryphal acts of Paul and Thecla, Peter, Andrew, John, and Jude Thomas, in *New Testament Apocrypha,* 2 vols., eds. William Schneemelcher and Edgar Hennecke (Philadelphia: Westminster Press, 1963).

ticulars of specific heterosexual relationships (Chapter 6) however, it is necessary to define the basic characteristics of Christian asceticism, and particularly celibacy, the phenomenon which made such friendship possible.

The importance of asceticism lay in its capacity to free individuals from those bodily pleasures which separated them from intimacy with God. Celibacy emerged as the most powerful ascetic practice, capable of establishing human contact with the divine. The Romans of Late Antiquity (second to the fourth century C.E.) were familiar with the notion of friendship with divinity and used it effectively as legitimation for extending power over their neighbors.[11] In the same vein the early Christians believed that martyrs had a special claim to friendship with God. According to Peter Brown,

> The Christians admired their martyrs because they had made themselves the "friends of God"; they summed up in their persons the aspirations of a group made separate from, and far superior to, their fellow men by reason of a special intimacy with the divine.[12]

When the monastic celibates replaced the martyr as the paradigmatic figure for attainment of salvation, the monastics became the special "friends of God." And since the communal way of life stripped them of the normal social supports of identity (husband and wife in marriage), they developed a substitute, a new paradigm, that of heterosexual friendship. As "friends of God" the monastics enjoyed a power which set them above the normative system of social arrangements and allowed for amiable interchanges between individual "friends." On the broader level the concept legitimated the minimization of racial, social, and sexual differentiation in that friendship with God made divine power accessible to any Christian.

That celibacy was the source of freedom which evoked communication between non-married men and women is recorded in the story of Sisinnius, "a slave by birth, though a free man in the faith."[13]

---

11. I am particularly indebted to Peter Brown's analysis in "The Friends of God," *The Making of Late Antiquity* (Cambridge: Harvard University Press, 1978), pp. 54–80.

12. *Ibid.*, p. 56.

13. *Laus. Hist.*, p. 186.

Sisinnius, a disciple of the ascetic master, Elpidius, shut himself in a grave for three years, then returned to his country, Cappadocia, where he established a community for celibate men and women. The success and excellence of the community was attributed to the fact that Sisinnius "trampled upon the lust which is in men, and he hath bridled the voluptuousness of the women, so that there hath been fulfilled that which is written, 'In Christ Jesus there is neither male nor female' (Galatians 3:28)."[14] That the presence of Christ within the ascetic allowed the freedom to express affection for others is likewise stated in the anecdote about Talida, head of a house of celibate women. Palladius went to visit her convent in Antinoe and was astonished to find that Talida had arrived at such a state of *"apatheia"* (freedom from or insensibility to sensual appetites) that "when I entered into her presence and sat down by her side, she stretched out her hands and laid them upon my shoulders, in the boldness and freedom which she had acquired in Christ."[15]

The ascetics' freedom to participate equally as "friends of God" in the pursuit of perfection constituted the legitimation for friendship between individuals. The sharing of mutual ideals and goals fostered the development of amicable relationships between Christian ascetics, especially between those who joined the monastic communities of the fourth to the sixth century. The majority of instances of heterosexual friendships is contained in literature about or correspondence between Church officials and women who were devoted to Church ministry and/or who were members of celibate women's communities. It is within the content of this literature that heterosexual friendship is most explicitly defined and demonstrated. Information about the origins of the ascetic monastic life (i.e., communal, rather than eremitic or solitary) provides clues to the reasons for celibacy's unique role in the potential relationships.

According to Palladius, Pachomius was advised by an angel to gather together those ascetics who were wandering about the countryside of Thebes, whereupon Pachomius dutifully established a monastery for men on the banks of the Nile at Tabennisi. Whether Pachomius founded a similar one for women or whether such were

---

14. *Idem.*
15. *Ibid.*, p. 153.

already in existence, Palladius mentions in passing that any surplus commodities which the monks had from their work were shared with the convents in the area. He adds that there were many nuns living on the opposite bank and beyond who followed this same rule for life. Whenever any one of them or any married woman died, the women would bring her to the bank of the river where certain monks would cross over, and with lighted candles and singing of psalms would escort the body across the Nile for burial in their cemetery.[16]

That such monastic communes were sometimes established by ascetics who had first been trained under the guidance of some spiritual master in the ascetic life is evidenced by another anecdote narrated by Palladius. Ammonius, his three brothers and two sisters, disciples of the ascetic master, Pambo, "when they had attained unto the perfection of divine life and conversion they departed from the desert and founded two monasteries, I mean, one for men and one for women, but they placed the monastery of the women at a sufficient distance from that of the men, for Ammonius did not greatly love the intercourse of speech."[17] Anthony, as mentioned previously, upon renouncing the world placed his sister, for whom he was responsible, in a "house of virgins."[18] Since there is not much information about such groups of celibate men prior to this period it seems plausible that groups of celibate women were established prior to those of men.

Many of these celibate women lived together in the homes of the more influential and affluent women, or in residences established by others interested in their welfare. The ascetic Elias, for example, was a friend of many such celibate women in the city of Thebes and Atrepe. He built a large home and gathered together about three hundred of them to form a communal way of life. Since he was fairly wealthy he provided for all their needs "with great zeal and care, for our Lord's sake."[19]

Many of the women's communities were founded by women who themselves had chosen to live the ascetic life. The noble Roman matron, Paula, and her daughter, Eustochium, personal friends of

---

16. *Ibid.,* pp. 146–47.
17. *Ibid.,* p. 105.
18. *Vita Ant.* 3.
19. *Laus. Hist.,* p. 143.

Jerome, established three convents at Bethlehem which enrolled many ascetic women and served as model for the founding of similar establishments.[20] A short time later Melania the Elder and her granddaughter established a convent on the Mount of Olives in Jerusalem at about the same time as Basil established one for his mother and sister, Macrina.[21] The number of these celibates was considerable. At Oxyrhyncus alone (near Cairo) there were twenty thousand nuns, and in quick succession equally prolific establishments sprang up in other parts of Egypt, Syria, Palestine, Asia Minor and Rome.[22]

The option of celibacy provided new possibilities for the Christian woman. Hilpisch summarizes the effect for women who chose to live the celibate life.

Under the influence of the religious fervor of the fourth century, thoroughly ascetic in character, enthusiasm for the ideal of consecrated virginity resulted in a powerful Christian women's movement, which attracted the noblest souls of the time. These women were concerned . . . with the fulfillment of womanhood through intellectual and spiritual values.[23]

To remain unmarried was no longer considered a disgrace or a misfortune; on the contrary, celibacy attained a position of prominence which at times had the unfortunate effect of depreciating marriage.

Celibacy granted to its female adherents a dignity and respect dependent not upon the wealth and position of a mortal husband, but upon identification with Christ to whom the celibate was symbolically espoused. The Song of Songs' celebrative attitude toward sensual pleasures became for the celibates symbolically representative of the joy and freedom possible through the individual's spiritual nuptials with Christ. In a spiritual or mystic sense Christ became surrogate bridegroom for celibate women, and surrogate bride for celibate men.

20. Jerome, *Ep.* 108, PL 22:896–906.

21. *Vita Macrinae,* PG 46:959–1000.

22. *Laus. Hist.,* p. 338.

23. Stephanus Hilpisch, *History of Benedictine Nuns,* trans. Sister M. Joanne Muggli (Collegeville, Minn.: St. John's Abbey Press, 1958), p. 8.

The erotic imagery of the Song of Songs had traditionally symbolized the great love between Yahweh and his bride Israel.[24] The New Testament appropriation of that theme was best developed in the writings of John and Paul which speak of the spiritual nuptials of the *Ecclesia* with Christ.[25] The Church as *sponsa Christi* ("spouse of Christ") became an integral part of the mystic theology of the Fathers of the Church.[26] And as the Church/bride was made up of its many members, so the individuals by means of rebirth through baptism were symbolically espoused to Christ. Thus symbolic language ("put aside the old man," "put on the new," "clothed with Christ," etc.[27]) and ritual acts (cleansing through the waters of baptism, stripping of old clothes, putting on the white baptismal robe) signified the salvific process of the Christians' "putting on Christ," i.e., becoming friends of the Son of God.[28] It is possible that the conviction of rebirth in Christ at baptism caused Paul to speak of the abandonment of racial, social, and sexual differentia in his famous, "All baptized in Christ, you have all clothed yourselves in Christ, and there are no more distinctions between Jew and Greek, slave and free, male and female, but all of you are one in Christ Jesus."[29]

The spiritual rebirth of the Christian through baptism did not, however, assure salvation. Baptism as a restoration of the Christian's integrity was a beginning, but spiritual perfection required a continued growth which the ascetic in particular struggled to attain. Hence

24. For a study of the Jewish allegorical interpretations of the Song of Songs, see Josephine Massyngberde Ford, *A Trilogy on Wisdom and Celibacy* (Notre Dame, Indiana: University of Notre Dame Press, 1967), pp. 104–26.

25. Rev. 19:7 and 21:9–10; 2 John 1 and 5; Rom. 7:2–4; Eph. 5:23–33; 2 Cor. 11.2–4. For an historical study of the development of the theme, see Claude Chavasse, *The Bride of Christ: An Enquiry into the Nuptial Element in Early Christianity* (London: Faber and Faber, 1940), pp. 127–34 and Joseph C. Plumpe, *Mater Ecclesia: An Inquiry into the Concept of the Church as Mother in Early Christianity* (Washington, D.C.: Catholic University of America Press, 1943).

26. Representative texts include: SH 4.2; Justin Martyr, *Dial. cum Tryph.* 63.4; Tertullian, *Adv. Marc.* 3.5, 4.11, 5.12 and 18; *De Exhort. Cast.* 5; *De Monog,* 5 and 13; *De Fuga* 14; *De Pud.* 1.8; Clement, *Paed.* 1.5.21; Origen, *De Orat.* 17.2; *In Matt.* 17.21; and *In Cant. Cant.* 1.8.

27. Gal. 3:28; Col. 2:9 and 3:10; Eph. 4:22.

28. Methodius, *Sympos.* 3.4, 8 and 9; Irenaeus, *Adv. Haer.* 1.2; and Tertullian, *De Anima* 43. Arthur Vööbus, in *Celibacy, A Requirement for Admission to Baptism in the Early Syrian Church* (Stockholm: n.p., 1951) provides evidence that in Syria as late as the fourth century celibacy was required of those wishing to be baptized.

29. Gal. 3:28. Cf. 1 Cor. 12:13; Col. 3:11; and Methodius, *Sympos.* 8.8.

the language and ritual of baptismal reunification became in a special sense the language and ritual of the struggles involved in the ascetic's dying daily.

The practice of celibacy, like baptism, served as an important symbol with Christianity of the unification of opposites through friendship with Christ.[30] The task of "making the two one" (especially male and female) in order to enter the kingdom is a prominent theme, for example, in the Gnostic *Gospel of Thomas* and other apocryphal works reflecting encratite Christianity of the East, particularly of eastern Syria.[31] Much of the literature dealing with the theme of unification of opposites tends to be highly mystical in character and unclear as to exact meaning or intent. Nonetheless the importance which the texts accord to celibacy as source of spiritual unification of the opposites, male and female, helps to clarify or explain celibacy's central position in the life of the ascetic/monastic.

According to the *Gospel of Thomas,* the *monachoi* (those who had attained "oneness" or "self-unity") were the only ones who would enter the bridal chamber, a locus symbolizing complete union with the Logos or Word of God (Christ the Son).[32] According to Meeks, there are similar motifs in the apocryphal Acts which stem from encratite circles:

> The virgin, Thecla, for example, could be taken as the very model of a female who "makes herself male," represented

30. See Wayne A. Meeks, "The Image of the Androgyne," 165–208. For a fuller treatment of early Christian views on celibacy see Ford, *A Trilogy;* Peter Harkx, *The Fathers on Celibacy* (De Pere, Wisconsin: St. Norbert Abbey Press, 1968); Sister M. Rosamund Nugent, *Portrait of the Consecrated Woman in Greek Christian Literature of the First Four Centuries* (Washington, D.C.: Catholic University of America Press, 1941); Francisco Vizmanos, *Las virgenes christianas de la iglesia primitiva* (Madrid: Editorial Catolica, 1949).

31. Cf. Clement of Alexandria, *Strom.* 3.13; 2 Clement 12.2; *Acts of Peter* 38; and *Acts of Philip* 140. For recent interpretations of Gnostic writings which deal with the male/female categories see Elaine Pagels, *The Gnostic Gospels* (New York: Random House, 1979), pp. 48–69 and "The Gnostic Vision," *Parabola* (November 1978), 6–9.

32. *Gospel of Thomas* 75. Compare this text to the admonition in the *Gospel of Philip* 73 that only "free men and virgins" can enter the bridal chamber. This is related to Philo's philosophical use of the phrase "making the female male" which depicts the wise man's progression through virtue and contemplation to a heightened self-awareness leading ultimately to *visio dei,* the culmination of philosophical perfection. An interesting study of his use of the terms "male" and "female" is found in Richard A. Baer, Jr., *Philo's Use of the Categories Male and Female* (Leiden: Brill, 1970).

in the story by her wish to cut her hair short and her donning of men's clothing, thus becoming what the Gospel of Thomas would call a *monachos*—not only a celibate, but also one who must break all ties to home, city, and ordinary society, becoming a wanderer. In the Encratite Acts, the ascetic life is idealized as that of an itinerant, whose baptism liberates him from "the world," understood primarily as sexuality and society. So also in the Gospel of Thomas, "becoming a single one" involves a radical separation from settled life: hatred of family, including not only marriage but also recognition of parents; perceiving the world as a "corpse"; and rejecting trade and commerce. Thus in these circles the union of male and female represents not a heightened or even a spiritualized libido, but a neutralization of sexuality, and therewith a renunciation of all ties which join the "unified" individual with society.[33]

The work's emphasis on the neutrality of sexuality and renunciation of all ties with society indicates regulatory themes which loom large in the traditions of both the Christian eremitic and monastic way of life. Although this work, like others of a similar nature (e.g., the *Shepherd of Hermas*), presents no direct information about the practice of celibacy in the early Church, the language of the allegorical personification of wisdom as female virgin may have influenced the later patristic development of a theology of celibacy. A seventh century work of Maximus the Confessor, for example, indicates the continuity of certain Gnostic and encratite teachings. In speaking of the various unions (*henoseis*) of the separated creatures which Christ effected, Maximus transfers the Gnostic emphasis on wisdom's effective centrality to the person of Christ. He says of Christ:

For he unified man by mystically abolishing through the Spirit the difference between male and female. In place of the two with their respective passions he constituted one which was free in respect to nature.[34]

---

33. *Op. cit.,* pp. 196–97.
34. *Quaestiones ad Thalassium* 48; PG 90:436.

That spiritual perfection (metaphorically expressed by the union of opposites, particularly male and female) was more easily accessible through celibacy than through marriage was expressed by an increasing number of later Christian writings. Athenagoras, for example, after addressing himself to the rewards of chaste wedlock, presented the claim that the indulgence of carnal thought and desire led away from God while virginity led toward God. In his view the "hope of living in closer communion with God" and the Christians' intent on action rather than on words had induced many Christian men and women to remain unmarried. He identified Christ's message about "eunuchs for the kingdom of heaven" (Mt. 19:11–12) as the scriptural validation of celibacy.[35] Several other apologists referred to continence and those subscribing to its practice, but there is no strong advocacy of celibacy as opposed to marriage.

Clement of Alexandria was one of the first to devote a major part of a work to the topic. Most of his chapter on celibacy was a refutation of heresies which disparaged marriage and indicated Clement's belief that both the celibate life and marriage were viable means of salvation.[36] With Origen there is a definite prominence already accorded celibacy and virginity. He concluded that virginity was first in rank among the sacrifices of life one could offer to God, being careful, however, to insist that it was not the only offering a Christian could make.[37] In another commentary he ascribed to virgins the distinct honor of being the first fruits of the Church, which indicated that more Christians were already embracing celibacy as a life-style.[38]

Tertullian's treatises on celibacy stressed the permissibility of marriage but left no doubt of the superior value he placed on continence. A major motif of his works was the plea to widows and widowers to maintain celibacy rather than remarry. In one treatise he classified second marriage as a kind of adultery,[39] while in two later

---

35. *Supp.* 33. Cf. I *Clem.* 38; Ignatius, *Ad Poly.* 5; and Justin Martyr, *Apol.* 29.

36. *Strom.* 3. For a fuller exposition of the scriptural proof texts supporting both the heretics' and Clement's views, see Ford, pp. 146–53.

37. *Ad. Rom.* 9.

38. *In Num. Hom.* 11. Contrast this with Tertullian's view in *Exhort. Cast.* 1.4 of the greater merit of celibate widowhood because it was a sacrifice of something already experienced.

39. *De Exhort. Cast.* 9.

works he completely condemned second marriages.[40] In Tertullian's literary attempts to dissuade others from remarriage, he posited as reasons the permanence of the marriage contract which in his view endured even after death, and the spiritual affinity between Christian brothers and sisters which made remarriage an incestuous union.[41] Tertullian's adoption of the Montanist sect which condemned marriage as an evil undoubtedly influenced his views.[42]

From the time of Tertullian on, there was a proliferation of literature dealing with celibacy and virginity as the most effective way of identification with Christ.[43] By the middle of the third century celibacy had attained great prominence, and celibate ascetics comprised a notable section of the Christian communities. Cyprian's eulogy expressed the prevailing notion that the ascetics stood as giants among the other Christians: "They are the flower of the ecclesiastical seed, the grace and ornament of spiritual abilities . . . the more illustrious portion of Christ's flock."[44]

In response to certain Jewish criticism of Christian celibacy, Aphrahat, a fourth-century Christian monk of Mesopotamia, defended virginity as a "gift for which there is no equivalent in the whole world."[45] In the Pauline tradition Aphrahat asserted that though marriage was good, celibacy was better in that it allowed the individual to honor God with undivided love. By a stretch of the historical imagination, he attempted to demonstrate that even in ancient times virginity as a means of sanctity was preferable to marriage: the heroes, Joshua, Elijah, and Elisha, did not marry; Moses refrained from "the duties natural to marriage" after his call from God; and Ezekiel was favored by widowhood when God "took and threw off from him the injurious yoke."[46] It was only when man became enam-

40. *De Monog.* and *De Pud., passim.*

41. *De Exhort. Cast.* 11.

42. See Ford, pp. 165–89, for a study of Phrygian Montanism's influence on Tertullian's views on celibacy.

43. Ford, pp. 230–33, presents a table showing the literary increase of works dealing with virginity and celibacy from I *Clement* to Jerome.

44. *De Hab. Virg.* 3, PL 4:455.

45. Jacob Neusner, *Aphrahat and Judaism: The Christian-Jewish Argument in Fourth-Century Iran* (Leiden: E. J. Brill, 1971), p. 83.

46. *Ibid.,* pp. 80–81. Cf. 1 Cor. 7:1 and 25–40.

ored of the opposite sex (and lost his virginity) that his heart turned from God and evil gained control.[47]

The extensive corpus of literature of this nature helped create a rhetorically idealized, conventional picture of the celibate male and female consecrated to Christ and/or God. There developed an elaborate and varied imagery depicting celibates as brides of Christ, beloved of God, spiritual athletes, brothers and sisters of saints, mothers and fathers of spiritual sons and daughters, etc., all indicative of a special relationship between God and individuals who were thereby gifted with special powers. One of these powers was fortuitously realized in the lives of many of the individuals, i.e., the power of mobility outside the normative structures of society. Heterosexual friendship was one of the indices of that mobility. Though such relationships were previously not a cultural characteristic, they became a paradigmatic observable phenomenon during the fourth, fifth, and sixth centuries. The direct and conclusive evidence about this phenomenon is not to be found in philosophic, theoretical literature on the subject, but in the *Vitae* of and correspondence between celibate men and women living in some type of monastic community.

---

47. *Ibid.*, pp. 81–82.

CHAPTER SEVEN

Celibacy and the Friendship Ideal

If there is any one image within Christian literature of the fourth and fifth centuries which articulates the rationale for heterosexual friendship it is the image of the ideal woman celibate. The proliferation of literature which expounds the virtues of these celibate women and outlines prescriptive details for their walk, speech, dress, food, and demeanor demonstrates the need of the times to create a separate space for a group outside the normative structures of society. The rise of celibate asceticism allowed women and men to reject the designated sexual roles of society and create a social system supportive of a new way of life. Heterosexual friendship developed in response to the need for reciprocal support in realizing the mutual goals of ascetic endeavors. Literature of the period confirms that generally only those women who were dedicated to pursuing the "angelic life" could transcend their allotted roles to participate in other forms of ministry and a type of male/female relationship other than that of marriage.

The ideal type of woman celibate as described in the *Vitae,* letters, and treatises of the Church Fathers was that of spouse of Christ (*sponsa Christi*), the Christian woman most clearly reflecting the image of God. Woman by nature was considered in greater need of redemption because of her "natural" condition as sinner, a symbol of carnality.[1] Hence, woman was in greater need of ascetic practice to

---

1. Rosemary Ruether traces the Christian development of this concept in "Misogynism and Virginal Feminism in the Fathers of the Church," *Religion and Sexism: Images of Woman in the Jewish and Christian Traditions* (New York: Simon and Schuster, 1974), pp. 150–83. Cf. Sheila Collins, *A Different Heaven and Earth* (Valley Forge: Judson Press, 1974), pp. 73–89.

make her "manly," and the more she became like the male the greater was her chance of salvation.[2] Therefore it was even more important for woman to transcend her sexuality and become like Pelagia, "a woman in sex, but not in spirit."[3] In so doing woman was allowed certain privileges not enjoyed by her married counterparts. One of these privileges was communication with celibate men who, like her, were exempt from certain normative restrictions.

The *Vitae* and letters of the Cappadocian Fathers (Basil the Great, Gregory Nazianzen, and Gregory of Nyssa) and John Chrysostom represent the view that woman's symbolic marriage with Christ exempted her from being cast so strictly in the role of temptress and seducer.[4] Consequently certain women relatives and friends of these writers were immortalized by their heavenly betrothals which produced extraordinary virtues that at times excelled those of their male counterparts. The very fact that certain women were granted literary recognition by male authors indicates a shift in the specific society's estimation of women's capabilities. Two works indicating this shift in view are funeral orations by the two Gregorys in honor of their sisters. Though the laudatory nature of the specific genre (panegyric) accounts for much of the emphasis on the excellent character and achievements of the sisters, the fraternal admiration

---

2. See particularly Elaine Pagels' interpretation of the Gnostic texts which deal with this topic, in "The Gnostic Vision," *Parabola* 3 (November, 1978), 6–9. Cf. the martyrdom account of Perpetua who in a vision became male as she prepared for battle with the devil in *Acts of the Christian Martyrs,* ed. and trans. Herbert Musurillo (Oxford: Clarendon Press, 1972), p. 119, and Amma ("mother") Sarah in the desert who rebuked her "brothers" with, "It is I who am the man, and you who are women," *The Sayings of the Desert Fathers,* trans. Benedicta Ward (London: A. R. Mowbray, 1975), p. 193. Several apocryphal works, particularly those of certain Gnostic Christians who were later rejected as heretical, emphasize the female's need to become male in order to acquire salvation. See particularly Elaine Pagels, *The Gnostic Gospels* (New York: Random House, 1979), pp. 48–69.

3. John Chrysostom, *De S. Pelagia* 2, PG 50:585.

4. See Rosemary Ruether, "Mothers of the Church: Ascetic Women in the Late Patristic Age," in *Women of Spirit: Female Leadership in the Jewish and Christian Traditions,* eds. Rosemary Ruether and Eleanor McLaughlin (New York: Simon and Schuster, 1979), pp. 72–98, and Elizabeth A. Clark, "Sexual Politics in the Writings of John Chrysostom," *Anglican Theological Review,* LIX (1977), 3–20. The earlier designation of the Christian virgin as bride of Christ is found in a treatise by Tertullian (*De Orat.* XXII, PL 1:1296–97). See John Bugge's study of the subject in *Virginitas: An Essay in the History of a Medieval Idea* (The Hague: Martinus Nijhoff, 1975), pp. 59–79.

stems from the sisters' commitment to the ascetic life.

One of the more complete biographies containing many of the conventional traits of the celibate Christian woman is that of Macrina, sister of Basil the Great and Gregory of Nyssa. It is an eloquent panegyric of the fourth century written *in memoriam* by her brother, Gregory.[5] Macrina is portrayed as a spirited, dynamic individual whose leadership potential was effectively realized within her own family, within the community of celibate women over which she presided, and within the associations of acquaintances from the community at large. She had an excellent intellectual training, particularly in scriptural studies. At the age of twelve her father had arranged for her to be married to a young nobleman who died before the marriage took place. Macrina decided to dedicate her life to God in perpetual celibacy and accordingly took great pains to discipline herself by certain ascetical practices. Gregory narrated how her life was spent in constant tears of repentance, prayer, fasting, silence, but particularly in the guarding of the senses, modesty, and contempt for adornment. So intent was she on having no adornment for her body that at her death her community could find among her possessions no garb for burial.[6] But in spite of these listings of conventional traits, Macrina still appeared as a strong-willed person not having to compromise her individuality as she demonstrated her ability to lead.

She had a great influence on her younger brothers, making herself personally responsible for their training in the scriptures and tenets of the Christian religion. When her father died, Basil convinced his mother and Macrina to go to Pontus where on a family estate they established a community of celibate women which was guided first by her mother, then at her death by Macrina. According to Gregory, Macrina led "the large number of virgins she had gathered about her in the way of perfection," regarding them as her daughters by a spiritual birth, and in motherly fashion caring for all their needs.[7] So famous was her reputation for generosity and concern for

5. *Vita Macrinae,* PG 46:959–1000. An English translation is that of W. K. Lowther Clarke, *Saint Gregory of Nyssa, The Life of Saint Macrina* (London: SPCK, 1916).

6. PG 46:990–91. Cf. Gregory Nazianzen's description of her in *Carmen* 120, PG 38:75.

7. PG 46:970–71.

others that her dwelling became "not a place of solitude, but a city."[8]
During her final illness her peaceful awaiting of death revealed to
those around her the love of her spiritual bridegroom, a love "con-
cealed and nourished within her soul."[9] Gregory's conclusion enu-
merated countless miracles attesting to the sanctity of his sister who
even while on earth had lived the "angelic life."[10] The characteristics
most frequently emphasized are those which stand in most apparent
contradiction or contrast to qualities usually ascribed to women
(e.g., great intelligence and learning, leadership, active engagement
in public and private works of charity).[11] And if female bodily images
were incorporated, it was with mystical or symbolic intent, so that
woman as bride, mother, servant became "bride of Christ," mother
of a "chorus of virgins begotten by a spiritual birth," and "your
handmaid" (the Lord's).[12] So "other-worldly" was the life of the virgin dedicated to God that "one could see the mouth practicing only
the law, the ear listening only to divine things, the hand ready for all
commands."[13] Freed from the pleasures of the senses which detract-
ed from perfection, the virgin was in a unique and privileged position
that made her appear less a temptress and more a teacher and spiritual guide whose presence in person or by correspondence provoked
emulation rather than temptation. Gregory dedicated his dialogue,
On the Soul and Resurrection, to Macrina, who is referred to
throughout as "the teacher." As such she is both the protagonist and
the one who clarifies for her brother the apparent contradictions and
confusions of the basic issues involved.[14] Christianity's message of
spiritual equality was Chrysostom's justification for women transcending their inferior position. He explained that not until Christ
appeared did women begin to surpass men in sanctity, fervor, devotion, and love of God.[15]

---

8. *Ibid.,* 971–72.
9. *Ibid.,* 984.
10. PG 46:992–96, 969–70, and 975–76. Cf. *Vita S. Syncleticae,* PG 28:1486–
1558, a work wrongly attributed to Athanasius. The account has features strikingly
similar to the stories of Macrina and Gorgonia.
11. PG 46:978, 984, 988.
12. *Ibid.,* 984, 977–78.
13. Gregory of Nyssa, *Ep.* 19, PG 46:1076. Cf. *Vita,* 969 and 972.
14. PG 46:11–160.
15. Homily 13, PG 62:99.

Another funeral oration from approximately the same period and same geographical region is that of Gorgonia, the sister of Gregory Nazianzen. Written in much the same vein as Gregory of Nyssa's panegyric on Macrina, it is nevertheless worthy of special recognition because of its analysis of both the married and the celibate states. Gorgonia was especially worthy of praise, according to Gregory, because she had chosen the better of two worlds, that of both the married and the unmarried states.

> The latter is loftier and more divine, though more difficult and dangerous; the former is more lowly but more safe. She was able to avoid the disadvantages of each and to select and combine everything best in both . . . blending the excellence of the married with that of the unmarried state, and proving that neither of them absolutely binds us to, or separates us from, God or the world (so that one because of its very nature would have to be avoided; the other wholly praised). But it is the mind which nobly presides over marriage and virginity, and forms and works on both as the raw material of virtue under the expertise of reason.[16]

Gregory then relates how Gorgonia had married but had eventually consecrated herself to God: "But what is most marvelous and admirable, she also won her husband to her way of thinking, and made of him a good co-worker rather than a domineering master."[17] The "fair harvest she had reaped" (three daughters and two sons) allowed her the opportunity to exemplify to the highest possible degree the noble household woman of Proverbs 31:10.[18]

Like Macrina she controlled her senses and refused ornament and display which produced a "cheap beauty of the infernal creator who works against the divine."[19] The only colors she would use in preserving "that image which should be kept for God and the world to come" were the red blush of modesty and the white of temperance.[20]

---

16. *Vita Gorgoniae* 8, PG 35:798, hereafter cited as VG, with page numbers in PG 35.

17. *Idem.*

18. VG 9:797.

19. VG 10:800.

20. *Idem.*

Gorgonia, like Macrina, had received an excellent intellectual training which, along with her native talent, gave her recognition "as a common advisor not only by the family members, those of the same people and the one fold, but even by neighboring people who accepted her counsels and advice as established laws not to be broken."[21] Her regular works of mercy are duly catalogued but do not evoke Gregory's wonder as did her ascetic practices. She regulated her life "as if freed from the body" and "in this respect she was seen to surpass not only women but the most devout of men . . . by the bending of her knees which had grown hard and almost took root in the ground."[22]

After Gregory recounted the heroics of Gorgonia's ascetic practices he reminded his listeners that she was but a proof of the Pauline doctrine of equality (Gal. 3:28).

> O womanly nature surpassing that of man in the common struggle for salvation, and demonstrating that the distinction between male and female is one of body, not of soul! O baptismal purity! O soul in the spotless vessel of your body, the bride of Christ! O bitter eating! O Eve, mother of our race and of our sin! O subtle servant and death, overcome by her self-discipline! O self-emptying of Christ and form of a servant, and sufferings reverenced through her mortification![23]

So effective was Gorgonia's asceticism that she was able to overcome the faults of her female nature and diminish or eradicate the gap between the lower and the higher states. Gregory nowhere states that Gorgonia was less favored by the Lord because of her previous married state, but he does recount all the marvelous deeds occurring after her promise of celibacy and the undertaking of ascetic practices. He calls Christ "her beloved" and "her lover," for love of whom she desired "to fling away these fetters, and escape from the mire in which we spend our lives."[24]

---

21. VG 11:801.
22. VG 13:803.
23. VG 14:805.
24. VG 19:812.

Gregory refers to Gorgonia's spiritual father, Faustinus, as a close advisor to whom Gorgonia entrusted her confidences and exchanged mutual exhortations and encouragement. He was present at her death, and

> ... in this wonderful scene, carefully watching her he noticed that her lips were gently moving. He placed his ear to them (which his disposition and sympathy emboldened him to do). ... Under her breath she was repeating a psalm ... a testimony to the boldness with which she was departing.[25]

It is difficult to ascertain exactly how close the relationship between Faustinus and Gorgonia was, but the fact that Gregory mentions him twice as one who shared confidences with her that were little known to others intimates that a mutual trust and respect existed between them.[26] Her celibacy, her ascetic endeavors, and her works of charity all made Gorgonia a prime candidate for the type of Christian woman with whom men could become personal friends, particularly in this period of Christian history.

Gregory Nazianzen, in a letter to Gregory of Nyssa on the death of his sister, Theosebia, gives his reason for loving the deaconess:

> But what must we feel in the presence of a long prevailing law of God which has now taken my Theosebia (for I call her mine because she lived a godly life; for spiritual relationship is better than bodily)? Theosebia, the glory of the church, the adornment of Christ, the helper of our generation, the hope of woman. ... And do not wonder that I often invoke her name, for I rejoice even in the remembrance of the blessed one.[27]

The notion that spiritual excellence in a person (usually judged by degree of asceticism) removed the dangers inherent in normal male/female friendships is intimated by the accounts' emphasis on

---

25. VG 22:813 and 816.
26. VG 15 and 22:805 and 816.
27. *Ep.* 197, NPNF, Ser. 2.7, p. 462.

negation of or control over bodily appetites. To find the happy medium did not suffice in attempting to purge the body from all sensual appetites. The more severe the discipline, the greater the diminution of or the control over the passions which hindered progress toward perfection. Hence Gregory Nazianzen could argue for the superiority of spiritual relationships which presumed a mutual striving for freedom from bodily impulses. The imagery of the individual's detachment from the world was paralleled by the individual's attachment to the things of God. The negative emptying of self included the simultaneous positive action of "filling up" with the things of God, an analogy expressed by John the Baptist's, "He must increase; I must decrease."[28] It was not the emptying of self in order to create a vacuum, but an emptying to make room for the coming in of Christ with whom the ascetic/monastic needed to identify. And when the human and the divine met, the recipient of that meeting was empowered to function beyond the allotted boundaries. There was an expansion, or even a rupturing, of the normative spatial territory within which men and women could function. The existence of amicable relationships between men and women celibates was one of the observable new paradigms which developed as celibacy minimized the importance of the normative relationship, marriage.

The most direct evidence about heterosexual friendship among Christians of the fourth and fifth centuries is contained in correspondence between men and women involved in Church ministry or living the monastic life-style in communities of celibates. Though the letters indicate personal concern for individuals' spiritual progress and well-being, they equally demonstrate varying degrees of affection between sender and receiver. And though few extant letters were written by women, it is possible to perceive their reactions and responses from the content of the male correspondence.

The letters were frequently a response to specific issues and questions raised by women in their letters. The relationship in such instances was generally a teacher/pupil one. Basil, for example, explained to a certain widow that since her letter contained disconcerting information "about all that is in your mind, I am stirred to write back to you."[29] In a letter to a certain group of canonesses (*canoni-*

---

28. John 3.30. Cf. Gal. 2.20.
29. *Ep.* 174, NPNF, Ser. 2.8, p. 219. Cf. *Ep.* 297.

cae), women living in the vicinity of a specific church and dedicated to education and works of charity, he discussed questions raised at the Council of Nicea (e.g., the meaning of *homoousion* and Sabellius' way of identifying *hypostases*) since "these are the points on which I have heard you making inquiry."[30]

He indicated his personal interest in and friendship with one of those *canonicae* in particular, Theodora. They had evidently been corresponding but for some reason his letters were under surveillance. He apologized to Theodora for not having written more often, but justified his action on the grounds that certain ill-intentioned servants had handed the letters over to other people.

> Yet, whether I write or not, one thing I do without failing, and that is to keep in my heart the memory of your excellence, and to ask the Lord to grant that you complete the course of good living which you have chosen.[31]

His letters indicate that he felt a personal responsibility toward women dedicated to Church ministry, that many of these women were conversant with theological and doctrinal matters, and that it was possible to be a personal friend with women dedicated in some way to service of the Church.

The most illustrious and provocative evidences of heterosexual friendships of the late fourth and early fifth centuries are found in the letters of John Chrysostom and Jerome.[32] Of the 173 letters of the former, seventeen are written to a deaconess Olympias, the most eminent and (if the tone of the letters is a fair indication) the best loved of his female friends. Olympias' father, a count in the court of Emperor Theodosius, died when she was very young. She was conse-

---

30. *Ep.* 52.4. Cf. Sozomen, *Hist. Eccl.* 1.117; and Basil, *Ep.* 173 and 285.

31. *Ep.* 173, PG 32:647.

32. A recent study dealing with the question of how one reconciles the negative attitudes of Jerome and John Chrysostom with the fact that they both cherished long-lasting friendships with women is Elizabeth A. Clark's, *Jerome, Chrysostom, and Friends: Essays and Translations* (New York: Edwin Mellen Press, 1979), pp. 1–157. Clark concludes that both men exempted their women friends from the class of "femaleness," but also "the living reality of their friendships with women was in the vanguard of the theoretical baggage they dragged with them in their journey from the ancient world to the new age of larger opportunities and higher esteem for the female sex" (p. 79).

quently entrusted to the guardianship of an uncle, Procopius, a good friend of Gregory Nazianzen. She was married for two years when her husband died, and she refused to marry a second time. Emperor Theodosius, irritated by her refusal to marry someone he had chosen for her, ordered her property confiscated. He later relented, however, and Olympias was ordained a deaconess and devoted her wealth and energy to the service of the Church. She became a close friend of John Chrysostom, the bishop of Constantinople. From Sozomen's *History of the Church* it is possible to reconstruct the major events in the lives of both Chrysostom and Olympias after they met, and particularly the services Olympias rendered to Chrysostom after his exile from Constantinople to Armenia in C.E. 404.[33] Chrysostom poignantly expresses the mental and physical suffering each endured because of this exile and allows glimpses of the mutual affection which exacerbated the pain of separation.[34]

Olympias apparently could not conceal her anxiety and distress over the fact that many bishops and clergy harbored ill-will against Chrysostom because of his attempted reforms in the Church at Constantinople. Since the letters were written after Chrysostom's exile from Constantinople, the recurring theme of Olympias' sadness and dejection because of his sufferings loomed large. Chrysostom repeatedly questioned her as to the cause of her suffering and attempted to allay her fears by recalling precedents of similar perilous days in past history.[35] He reminded her that none of the present ills should cause her such concern since "there is only one thing, Olympias, which is really terrible, only one real trial, and that is sin."[36] He advised her to compare the misfortunes with the good things they had known in life

---

33. PG 67:1111–1286. See particularly Chapters 9, 22, 24, 27. Eastern women of nobility were frequently exempt from certain sexually-discriminatory restrictions. Cf. Claude Vatin, *Recherches sur le Mariage et la Condition de la Femme Mariee a l'Epoque Hellenistique* (Paris: E. DeBoccard, 1970), pp. 241–75; Joan Morris, *The Lady Was a Bishop* (New York: Macmillan, 1973), pp. 124–29; Grace H. McCurdy, "Queen Eurydice and the Evidence for Woman Power in Early Macedonia," *American Journal of Philology,* 48 (1927), 201–14 and Kenneth G. Holum, "Pulcheria's Crusade C.E. 421–22 and the Ideology of Imperial Victory," *Greek, Roman, and Byzantine Studies,* 18.2 (Summer 1977), 153–72.

34. PG 52:549–623. Hereafter the page references to Chrysostom's letters are from PG 52.

35. *Ep.* 1:534–35.

36. *Ibid.,* 549.

"so you may divert your mind from despondency and derive much consolation from the work."[37] He told her he would write longer letters if she wished it.

> For letters are an appropriate remedy for evoking cheerfulness in you, and you will continually receive letters from me. And when you write to me again do not tell me you have much comfort from my letters, because this I know by myself. But tell me that you have as much consolation as I wish for you, and that you are not upset because of depression, nor that you spend your time in weeping, but rather in serenity and happiness.[38]

In the next letter he chided her gently for allowing despondency to gain the upper hand in her life and thus pose a serious threat to her health.[39] He reminded her of the value of her celibacy, recounted her virtuous ascetic practices, recalled for her Job's victory in spite of suffering, and consoled her in her greatest grief, that of his absence.[40]

The recurring pattern of the letters included a review of Olympias' state of health as reported to him by herself and others, an occasional reference to his own condition, encouragement to subdue the sadness and grief she was experiencing, reminder by examples that good can be derived from evil, and the assurance of his continued concern for her well-being. He included a suggestion for the kind of medicine Olympias should use in her illness, and followed it by the request that she also arrange to send more of it to him.[41] At one point he intimated that she had not always taken his advice on patient endurance.

> Have I not often, both in person and through letters, discussed this theme with you? But since perhaps the pressures of business, or the peculiar nature of your sickness, and the rapid succession of changes in your condition do not permit you to retain in your mind what I have repeat-

---

37. *Ibid.,* 555.
38. *Idem.*
39. *Ep.* 2:556.
40. *Ibid.,* 568.
41. *Ep.* 4:590.

edly and clearly stated, listen once more while I try to heal the wounds of your despondency by repetition of the same remedies.[42]

He further reminded her that unless she tried to cure herself "from these dismal swamps of despondency in spite of the unlimited amount of advice and exhortation," he would not too readily continue his frequent and long letters. He concluded, "Therefore do not show me words but facts, and when you get well letters will again arrive exceeding the limits of former communications."[43]

Chrysostom's psychology apparently had its intended effect since he later congratulated Olympias on her release from illness and her renewed ability to accept the past and present misfortunes.

> Therefore I rejoice and jump for joy. I am in a flutter of delight and insensible to my present loneliness and other troubles surrounding me. I am cheered, light-hearted, and not in a little way proud on account of your greatness of soul, and the repeated victories which you have won. And this, not only for your own sake, but also for that large and populous city [Constantinople] where you are like a tower, a haven, and a wall of defense, speaking with the eloquence of example and through your sufferings instructing both sexes to strip readily for these contests ... and cheerfully bear the struggles which such contests involve.[44]

Chrysostom could not cease from her praise because, unlike others elated by such honors as are her due, "you, on the contrary, woman that you are, clothed with a fragile body ... have not only avoided falling into such a condition yourself, but have prevented many others from so doing."[45] She is then acclaimed as a living proof that

> ... the wrestlings of virtue do not depend on age or bodily strength, but only on the spirit and the disposition. ...

---

42. *Ibid.*, 591.
43. *Ibid.*, 595.
44. *Ep.* 6:599.
45. *Ibid.*, 600–01.

Therefore I rejoice and leap for joy. . . . So that although my separation from you distresses you, you nevertheless have this very great consolation evoked by your successful exploits. For I also, banished at such a great distance, gain no small joy for this reason, that is, from your courage.[46]

That the need for encouragement and consolation was reciprocal is indicated by Chrysostom's complaint to Olympias that among the many letters brought by friends there was none from her. His anxiety about her health forced him to inquire into the cause for her non-communication.[47]

That Olympias heeded Chrysostom's advice and was eventually released from her despondent moods seems plausible from Chrysostom's last extant letter to her. He wrote only praise as he acclaimed her perseverance, recounted her strengths, and predicted her further victories over any trials yet to occur.[48] And though he revealed his acceptance of a social prejudice by speaking of her "woman's body more feeble than a cobweb," he elevated her to an even greater position by describing her victories in all her former battles "by treading underfoot with derisive scorn the fury of lusty men gnashing their teeth at you."[49]

Since all of Chrysostom's extant letters were written during his exile, there is much repetition and great general similarity in content. But those to Olympias exhibit a natural, sometimes coaxing, teasing, almost playful style. Their general tone is one of warm affection for someone who was friend, mutual advisor, and defender of his policies and actions. That her suffering for the Church at Constantinople was chiefly due to Chrysostom's removal from that city's bishopric and his subsequent exile is indicated in almost each of the seventeen extant letters. The basic contents demonstrate the friends' mutual concern for each other's health and safety and the consolation derived from the interchange of correspondence.

---

46. *Idem.* Chrysostom's reference to Olympias' success may refer to her great loyalty to him when she was brought publicly before the prefect of Constantinople and accused of setting fire to the church from which Chrysostom was exiled. For Olympias' heroic self-defense, see Sozomen, *Hist. Eccl.* 24.

47. *Ep.* 10:609.

48. *Ep.* 17:621–23.

49. *Ibid.,* 622.

The rhetorical and sometimes flamboyant letters of Jerome emphasized and often exaggerated the importance allotted to celibacy and other ascetic practices. As a student of Gregory Nazianzen and an acquaintance of Gregory of Nyssa, he undoubtedly had opportunities to discuss, debate, and formulate opinions of his own regarding the relative merits of marriage versus celibacy.[50] There is little doubt from his writings that his predilections resided with the latter, since even his praise of marriage was contingent upon its fruitful issue:

> I praise marriage; I praise wedlock; but because they bear me virgins. I gather the rose from the thorn, the gold from the mire, the pearl from the shell.[51]

Approximately one-third of Jerome's letters were written to women, and of these an astonishing number have as their purpose to dissuade women from marriage and exhort them to celibacy. As friend and part-time secretary to Pope Damasus, Jerome made the acquaintance of many aristocratic elite in Rome. He consequently became counselor to many women from these elite families, women whose religious fervor and independence allowed them a life of asceticism within their homes or in small communities. Whether Jerome's extreme exaggerations of the evils of marriage and blessings of celibacy derived from personal views and/or frustrations or whether they were, as Ruether claims, "the rhetorical topoi of the overheated ascetical imagination" is not germane to the present study.[52] What is important is that the prolixity of his letters allows adequate opportunity to view the extent to which he was able to be friend and counselor to a variety of women on different levels of personal friendship.

Because of the extensive correspondence between Jerome and his women friends, it is necessary to limit the specific examples to those letters indicating his closest personal relationships. Although he cultivated close personal friendships with many ascetic women, three names in particular appear quite frequently in his correspondence: Paula, Marcella, and Eustochium. These three he regarded as

50. Jerome, *Ep.* 80 and 93, PL 22:733–35, 769–71; and *De Vir. Illus.* 128, PL 23:753–54. Hereafter the page references to Jerome's letters are from PL 22.

51. *Ep.* 22:405–06.

52. Rosemary Radford Ruether, "Misogynism and Virginal Feminism," p. 171.

peers and co-counselors in the pursuit of ascetic ideals. The fact that some of his critics accused him of less honorable intentions did not deter him from continuing the friendships, though he did reprimand other prelates and monks for enjoying equally intimate platonic relationships.[53]

In a letter to Ascella, one of Jerome's close friends within the ascetic circle of Roman women, he confided his great affection for Paula who was soon to follow him to Jerusalem.

> It often happened that I found myself surrounded by virgins. To some of them I interpreted the sacred books as well as I was able. Our studies effected continuous communication which soon ripened into intimacy and then produced mutual confidence. If they [critics] have ever seen anything in my conduct unbecoming a Christian, let them say it! . . . No, my sex was my only crime, and even on this score I am not attacked except when there is talk of Paula coming to Jerusalem. . . . Of all the ladies in Rome, only one had the power to subdue me, and that one was Paula. She mourned, fasted, was squalid with dirt, had eyes dim from weeping . . . the only woman who stole my fancy was one whom I had not even seen at table. But as I began to revere, respect, and venerate her as her outstanding chastity deserved, all my former virtues forsook me on the spot.[54]

This generous praise of Paula became even more extravagant in the literary tribute Jerome wrote to Eustochium at the death of Paula. Here Jerome sketched Paula as the ideal spiritual woman, i.e., the celibate ascetic and the "mother of virgins," the mother who both trained her own daughters in the ascetic ideal of life, and served as mother of a community of other celibate women.[55] Jerome related how after the death of her husband, Paula gradually decided to leave

---

53. Cf. *Ep.* 117:867; and 147:1195–1204. See J. N. D. Kelly, *Jerome: His Life, Writings, and Controversies* (New York: Harper and Row, 1975), pp. 91–103.

54. *Ep.* 45, PL 22:481–83. This is Paula the Elder, distinguishing her from her granddaughter, Paula, who later followed the Elder's way of life and is the object of the discussion in *Ep.* 107.

55. *Ep.* 108:878–906.

her home and, "alone and unaccompanied (if it could ever be said that she was so), to go to the desert made famous by its Pauls and Anthonys."[56] Leaving her five children behind, she sailed East to visit the cells of men and women celibates who, like her, had resolved to live the ascetic life. As her children stood on the shore weeping at her departure,

> Paula's eyes were dry as she turned them heavenwards. And she overcame her love for her children by her love for God. She knew herself no more as a mother, so that she might prove herself a handmaid of Christ. Yet her heart was rent and she wrestled with her grief as though torn from part of herself. The magnitude of the affection she had to overcome made everyone admire her victory even more.[57]

Paula made a tour of the groups of celibates, stopping at Cyprus for ten days to visit her friend, Epiphanius, and at Antioch where she was detained by another friend, Paulinus. At Nitria,

> . . . her enthusiasm was marvelous and her endurance scarcely credible in a woman. Forgetting her sex and her weakness, she even desired to settle there among those thousands of monks, together with the girls who accompanied her.[58]

However, she continued to Bethlehem where she decided to establish permanent residence. Within three years she had established a monastery for men (presided over by Jerome), one for women (presided over by herself), and a guest-house for passing travelers. Jerome tells how he continually advised and consoled her, discussed scriptural texts and interpretations, aided her in defending Church doctrine

---

56. *Ibid.,* 881.

57. *Idem.*

58. *Ep.* 108:890. See Rosemary Rader, "The Role of Celibacy in the Origin and Development of Christian Heterosexual Friendship," Diss. Stanford University, 1977, pp. 149–62, for a longer discussion of the pilgrimage of Paula and other ascetic women.

against heretics' questioning, and instructed her in Hebrew. And lest anyone accuse Jerome of exaggerating Paula's holiness, he called God to witness the truth of his statements.

> On the contrary, I tone down much so that I may not appear to relate absurdities. My gnawing critics, forever biting me as hard as they can, need not insinuate that I am drawing on my imagination or decking Paula, like Aesop's crow, with the fine feathers of other birds.[59]

In the same passage he indicated how closely she followed his advice on living the ascetic life: she was the least remarkable of her community in dress, speech, gesture, walk; never ate with a man; never bathed unless dangerously ill (reminding the less ascetic younger women that "a clean body and a clean dress mean an unclean soul"); slept on hard ground; prayed almost day and night; wept constantly over her sins; and was generous to a fault. She impressed upon her community members the same sort of discipline, and so effective was the message that "she divided into three companies and monasteries the numerous virgins whom she had gathered out of different provinces, some of whom are of noble birth while others belonged to the middle or lower classes."[60]

Jerome consoled Paula's daughter, Eustochium, in that through her mother she had a splendid heritage.

> The Lord is your inheritance; and to increase your joy your mother has now won her crown after a long martyrdom. It is not only the shedding of blood that is considered a confession; the spotless service of a dedicated mind is itself a daily martyrdom.[61]

So great was Jerome's grief at the death of Paula that he was

---

59. *Ibid.*, 890–91.

60. *Ibid.*, 897–98. In this section on the daily order of Paula's monastery, Jerome tells how she punished a frequent offender of the Rule by "placing her among the lowest of the sisters and outside their society," an indication that there was some rank or class distinction within the community. Apparently some women of the upper classes were reluctant or unwilling to relinquish their social status.

61. *Ibid.*, 905–06.

unable to write the encomium to Eustochium and had to dictate it. As often as he took up the pen his finger stiffened, his hand fell, and his control over writing failed. He concluded:

> And now, Paula, farewell, and with your prayers aid the old age of your supporter. Your faith and your works unite you to Christ, where standing in his presence you will easily acquire what you ask. I have built a monument more lasting than bronze, which no interval of time can destroy. And I have cut an inscription on your tomb ... so that wherever my narrative may go, the reader may learn that you are buried at Bethlehem and are remembered there with praise.[62]

Jerome's inconsolable grief at the death of Paula was partly assuaged by his affection for her daughter, Eustochium, who had gone to Bethlehem with her mother and succeeded her as head of the women celibates' community there. In his consolatory letter on the death of Paula, Jerome praised Eustochium's continuance of the good work initiated by her mother.

> The same accomplishments can be seen today in her daughter, Eustochium, who always kept close to her mother's side, obeyed all her orders, never slept apart from her, never went outside the monastic confines or took a meal without her, never had a cent that she could call her own, rejoiced when her mother gave Eustochium's patrimony to the poor, and fully believed that in filial affection she had the best heritage and the truest riches.[63]

In perhaps the most famous of Jerome's letters, he elaborated for Eustochium the motives for anyone's choice of celibacy and the rules by which that way of life should be regulated.[64] In it he calls Eustochium "my Eustochium, daughter, lady, fellow-minister, sister.

---

62. *Ibid.,* 906. Cf. *Ep.* 30, 33, 39, 46, and 99.

63. *Ep.* 108:903.

64. *Ep.* 22:394–425. Thirty years later Jerome wrote a letter (130) of the same nature to Demetrias.

These names refer to your age, rank, religious calling, and the last to my affection for you."[65] Throughout the letter he repeatedly reminded Eustochium of the ascetic discipline incumbent upon her as "bride of Christ."

> Lady Eustochium (for I am bound to call my Lord's bride, "Lady.")
> ... warning you as Christ's spouse to avoid wine as you would avoid poison.
> Why do you, God's bride, hurry over to visit the wife of a mere man?
> Christ's spouse ... should be the guardian of the law of the Lord.
> Let foolish virgins stray abroad, but for your part stay at home with the bridegroom.[66]

He goes so far as to bestow on the celibate women's mothers the title, "the mother-in-law of God."[67] As for the celibates themselves, they are to tell their critics, "For me, virginity is consecrated in the persons of Mary and of Christ."[68]

Jerome's seemingly exaggerated praise of virginity and celibacy was accentuated by his demeaning attitude to marriage as inherently polluting. Whether this was due to his memories of violent temptations against chastity in his own life,[69] or his predilection for asceticism and/or affection for the women celibates' choice of that state, he leaves no doubt that for him marriage was an inferior state. He went to great lengths to recount the drawbacks of marriage: "pregnancy, crying of infants, torture caused by a rival [woman], burdens of household management, and all those imagined blessings which death finally cuts short."[70] Speaking of Eustochium's sister, Blaesilla, who lost her husband after seven months, he bemoaned her condition in that "she has lost at the same time the crown of virginity and the pleasures of wedlock."[71] But worse still than the married state

65. *Ibid.,* 411.
66. *Ibid.,* 395, 399, 403, 410, and 412. Cf. 394, 397, 405, 411, 415, and 425.
67. *Ep.* 22:407.
68. *Ibid.,* 405.
69. *Ibid.,* 398–99.
70. *Ibid.,* 395.
71. *Ibid.,* 403.

was that of the virgin or celibate who had failed to retain that honored position.

> I will say it boldly, that though God can do all things he cannot raise up a virgin once she has fallen. He may indeed free her from punishment, but he will not give her a crown in her corrupt condition.[72]

He warned women celibates to shun the company of men and married women and choose instead "women pale and thin with fasting, approved by their years and conduct."[73] Men especially were to be avoided, since many feigned a sad exterior and pretended to fast while they feasted in secret. In one such cautionary passage Jerome indicates that celibates were allowed certain social privileges not accorded to others.

> There are others of my own rank who seek the priesthood and the diaconate simply that they may more easily see women. Such men think of nothing but their dress, use perfumes freely. . . . Their curly hair shows traces of the curling-tongs . . . they tiptoe across a damp road so as not to splash their feet. When you see men acting in this way, think of them more as bridegrooms than as clergymen.[74]

All of these temptations in the forms of seeming innocence were to be considered as part of the "many stratagems which the wily enemy employs against us."[75] But Jerome assured Eustochium that constantly being on one's guard assured success.

> To be like the martyrs, or the apostles, or Christ, involves a hard struggle, but brings with it a great reward. . . . Rejoice, my sister! Rejoice, my daughter! Rejoice my virgin! For you have resolved to be in reality what others insincerely pretend to be.[76]

---

72. *Ibid.,* 397.
73. *Ibid.,* 404.
74. *Ibid.,* 413–14.
75. *Ibid.,* 415.
76. *Ibid.,* 422–23.

Eustochium and Jerome were close, personal friends for over thirty-five years. That she assisted Jerome in his biblical work is attested by his attributing much of his literary success in biblical studies to her. In a letter to Laeta, the daughter of Paula and sister of Eustochium, concerning the education of her young daughter, Jerome advised that she hand the girl over to Eustochium "whose language, walk, and dress are an education in virtue," and who, along with Paula, had "mighty souls animating their small bodies."[77] Jerome stated that Eustochium's sudden death "has upset me terribly and almost changed my way of life, for old age is telling on me."[78]

Jerome's ascetic acquaintances were acclaimed as role models for other women. In a letter of guidance to a recently-widowed Roman, Furia, Jerome instructed her in the preservation of a chaste widowhood ("the second of the three degrees of chastity"[79]), presented Paula and Eustochium as "the fairest flowers of your stock," and praised Marcella as the type of saintly woman in Furia's city "whose example you may well imitate" because she "has set before us a life worthy of the gospel."[80] Of Jerome's letters to lady friends, seventeen were written to Marcella, one whom he affectionately considered teacher, counselor, and friend.[81]

After Marcella's death, Jerome wrote to console her dearest friend, Principia, a member of an order of sisterhood which Marcella had established on the Aventine in Rome.[82] He lamented that for two years he could not write about her death because of the incredible sorrow it caused him. He recounted her widowhood seven months after marriage, her decision to remain celibate, her renown in Rome both for her role as benefactor to many and as a scripture scholar, her founding of a monastic community in Rome for women, and her public and successful refutation of a heresy rampant in Rome. Since Jerome had left Rome for Bethlehem he had to rely on mutual correspondence to bridge the separation. He told of Marcella's and Principia's success in establishing the Aventine community.

77. *Ep.* 107:877.

78. *Ep.* 143:1181. Cf. *S. Hieronymi Vita* 10, PL 22:174.

79. *Ep.* 54:550–60. According to Jerome, the highest degree of chastity was the preservation of virginity; the third, a chaste marriage.

80. *Ibid.,* 550 and 560.

81. *Ep.* 23, 24, 25–29, 32, 34, 37, 38, 40–44, and 59.

82. *Ep.* 127:1087–95.

For a long time you lived together and because many ladies conducted themselves according to your example I had the joy of seeing Rome transformed into another Jerusalem. Monastic establishments for virgins became numerous, and of hermits there were countless numbers. In fact the servants of God were so numerous that monasticism which had before been a term of reproach subsequently became one of honor. Meantime we consoled each other in our separation by words of mutual encouragement. So we discharged in spirit the debt which we could not pay in person. Our letters always met as we tried to outdo each other in attentions and anticipated each other in courteous inquiries. Not much was lost by a separation so effectively bridged by a constant correspondence.[83]

His correspondence with Marcella was varied in content; some dealt with theological and doctrinal matters, others with events affecting their lives or those of other mutual friends. The general tone of the letters is one of respect and genuine affection for Marcella whom he praised as the first noblewoman in Rome to call herself a nun and establish in her home a religious community.[84] Though he encouraged her to join him and the women's celibate communities in Bethlehem, she chose to remain in Rome where she died a few days after Alaric's soldiers plundered her monastic home.

That Jerome was conscious of critics' reactions to his close friendships and eloquent praise of women friends is evident from the same letter to Principia. He defended himself on scriptural evidence.

The incredulous reader may perhaps laugh at me for dwelling so long on the praises of mere women; but he only need recall how holy women followed our Lord and savior and ministered to him of their resources. And if he remembers how the three Marys stood before the cross, and especially how Mary Magdalene . . . was privileged to see the rising Christ first of all before the apostles themselves, he will

83. *Ibid.*, 1092.
84. *Ibid.*, 1089.

convict himself of pride before convicting me of foolish-
ness. For we judge a person's virtues not by sex but by
character, and consider those who have renounced both
rank and wealth to be worthy of the greatest renown.[85]

That his emulation of the women was contingent upon their
having chosen the celibate life is demonstrated by his preoccupation
with the topic of ascetic practices and from the fact that his female
correspondence was almost entirely with celibate women living in
community. That he was particularly fond of Paula the Elder, Eustochium, and Marcella, and that he considered them spiritual and intellectual equals can be surmised from his questioning them on a
variety of scholarly topics and dedicating to them many of his literary works.[86] Although his literary views may not represent what he
consistently did in practice, they intimate that spiritual mastery and
excellence were levelers of sexual inequities. In his reminder to Demetrias to choose her friends wisely (and especially from among
chaste women) he claims, "It is a maxim of the world that the only
real friendship is one based on an identity of likes and dislikes,"[87]
hence his acceptance of celibate women as equals on the ascetics'
road to salvation.[88] In defending himself against those criticizing his
acquaintance with women and his ascetic recommendations, Jerome
reiterated the integrity of his relationships.

Except by letter we have no knowledge of each other; and
where there is no fleshly acquaintance religion alone is the
reason for communication.[89]

Though Jerome, like others since Origen's time, may justly be
accused of phantasizing celibacy as a spiritual relationship (cf., for
example, his frequent reference to the Song of Songs and the psalms),
it provided him with the motivation and spirit to work, pray, study,

---

85. *Ibid.*, 1090.
86. See for example, the list of dedications of Jerome's literary works in NPNF,
Ser. 2.6, pp. ix–x.
87. *Ep.* 130:1117.
88. Cf. *Ep.* 11, 13, 45, 54, 65, 75, 76, 78, 79, 117, 120, and 122. *Ep.* 118 and 122
are samples of Jerome's attempts to convince men to adopt the celibate life.
89. *Ep.* 54:550.

and correspond with women friends whom he considered equal and even superior in regard to ascetic prowess.

The fact that there were undoubtedly other letters which for some reason are no longer extant offers a clue to the extent to which early Christian men and women were able to relate on a more personal level. Although there was still the distinction between Church official and lay Christian (a distinction more recognizable as a stricter hierarchical structure developed after the fourth century) there was less emphasis on the matters which separated than on the bonds which united the members of the "body of Christ."[90] That women's choice of celibacy as a way of living the Christian life set them apart as somewhat superior or worthy of special consideration is evident throughout the bulk of correspondence. Celibacy thus became a means by which a less restrictive, more egalitarian type of relationship was able to exist between men and women. The correspondence reflects the attitude of the Church Fathers who, like Jerome, considered celibacy as characteristically a surpassing or negation of sexual differentiation. Jerome makes the distinction:

> For difference of sex while essential to marriage is not so to a celibate tie, since even in the flesh if we are born again in Christ we are no longer Greek and barbarian, slave and free, male and female, but are all one in him [Christ].[91]

The image of woman which emerges from a study of the *Vitae,* discourses on celibacy and virginity, and correspondence between men and women of the fourth and fifth centuries is that of the ascetic, spiritually-oriented, celibate woman who because of her chosen state occupied a position different from and superior to her married sexual counterparts. Ruether summarizes this shift in attitude:

> In this twilight period of antiquity, we see, then, the image of the virginal woman appearing as a new cultural ideal,

---

90. The same theme of unification in Christ is expressed in letters of a later period, but since the present study is limited to the period of the third through the fifth centuries, Jerome's letters serve as an appropriate *terminus ad quem.* Cf., however, Augustine, *Ep.* 92, 94, 127, 155, 183, 208, 210, 262, 267, etc.; and Gregory the Great, *Ep.* 4.30; 7.12 and 25; 10.15, 18, 19; and 11.35, 44, 78.

91. *Ep.* 75:686.

raising up the possibility of woman as capable of the highest spiritual development, which could lead to the *summum bonum* of communion with the divine intellectual nature of the Divine itself. Such heights had previously been reserved for men in antiquity, although the twilight of Neoplatonism also boasted a woman sage, Hypatia.[92]

The "new cultural ideal" of the celibate woman was the result of a progression in thought from the Church as spouse of Christ, to the individual as spouse through rebirth at baptism, to the celibate ascetic's special claim to the title by virtue of the practice of celibacy. By the celibate's mastery of the body's natural propensities to sins of the flesh a unification of opposites became possible. Hence male/female relationships were established on what often appeared as a denial of sexuality, but which were more positively viewed as a spiritual reciprocity of individuals whose identification with Christ minimized or attempted to obliterate the dangers of sexual attraction.

---

92. Ruether, "Misogynism and Virginal Feminism," p. 178.

CHAPTER EIGHT

Institutionalization of the
Friendship Ideal

With the exception of the martyr accounts, the majority of heterosexual friendships portrayed in Christian literature of the third, fourth, and fifth centuries occurred between celibate men and women. References to married individuals' participation are conspicuously absent. This apparent exclusivity occurred for a variety of reasons, but three are particularly discernible.

First, the nature of the literature itself limited the type of incidents recorded. When Christianity came into its own and expanded numerically and geographically, there developed a hierarchical structure with carefully delineated tasks and positions. With the increase of ecclesial bureaucracy there developed the need to preserve official data and dicta. The nature of the selection process dictated that the literary records preserved were those of officials, the elite of the administrative structure. The importance of the literary expression was directly equated with the importance of the position maintained by the individual authors. Hence, the records are almost solely those of bishops and other administrative officials whose communications were generally directed toward those with whom certain political or social relationships had been established. This explains the inestimable loss of correspondence of women and other minority members of society. We know, for example, from the extant correspondence of Augustine, Jerome, John Chrysostom, and others, that many women corresponded with them, but their letters were not preserved in spite of the fact that several of the women were deaconesses actively involved in official Church ministry. And if there was correspondence between Church officials and married women such communications may have been the first discarded in the selection process because of the women's non-official status.

Secondly, married women were by law, marriage custom, and religious precept subservient to and dependent upon their husbands for all of their needs. That they were allowed certain privileges in regard to communication from clerics who served as spiritual advisors is indicated by a canon of the Council of Elvira. The canon mandated that married women use their husbands' names to write to *lay* Christians, but were not to receive letters of friendship addressed only to themselves.[1] Furthermore, interests of conjugal fidelity required restrictions on a wife's amicable communications, though no mention is made of equal restrictions on husbands' correspondence. Thus, women as wives were by definition divorced from participation in activities conducive to close heterosexual friendships. Their sphere of influence was restricted to the confines of the home.

But the basic reason for the exclusivity of heterosexual friendship between celibates lay in the importance which the early Church allotted to celibacy. In imitation of the martyrs, the ascetics' dying daily to self tended toward a neutralization of sexuality, a minimization of the sexual differentiation generally experienced by the societies in which early Christians lived. According to John Chrysostom, it was virginity and celibacy which, like martyrdom, gave women the opportunity to rise above the limitations normally allotted to the female.[2] He asserted that the coming of Christ had effectively obliterated the discriminations of the past and allowed greater freedom for those confessing faith in Christ.[3]

As discussed in Chapter 3, Wayne Meeks argues that the elimination or minimization of sexual inequalities was part of a larger movement within the early Church which stressed unity through unification of opposites.[4] He cites the Nag Hammadi and other

---

1. Can. 81.

2. *In. S. Barlaam* 4, PG 50:682.

3. John Chrysostom, *De Virg.* 41, PG 48:563; *Hom.* 17 on *Matt.* 4, PG 57:259; *Hom.* 5 on *Gen.* 3, PG 54:602 and *Adv. Oppugnatores* 3.11, PG 47:366.

4. Wayne A. Meeks, "The Image of the Androgyne: Some Uses of a Symbol in Earliest Christianity," *History of Religions,* 13 (February 1974), 165–67.

Gnostic texts as sources which demonstrate that the notion of unification of opposites, "and especially the opposite sexes, served in early Christianity as a prime symbol of salvation."[5] Meeks suggests that Paul's narration of pairs of opposites in Galatians 3:28 is a direct quote from part of the baptismal ritual. This ritual symbolized a reunified humanity in which categorical distinctions (Jew/Greek, slave/free, male/female) were "mediated," i.e., reconciled through incorporation into the *ecclesia* as the earthly extension of Christ's body. According to Meeks, the unification theme "was not just pious talk in early Christianity, but a quite important way of conceptualizing and dramatizing the Christians' awareness of their peculiar relationship to the larger societies around them."[6]

Besides baptism there were various other ritualistic practices and customs which aided the mediation of opposites: e.g., the agape celebration; the kiss of peace; the common sharing of property; the appellation, "brothers" and "sisters." These practices set the Christians apart from the rest of their contemporaries and allowed the consideration of themselves as a new genus of mankind, a third race.[7] The concept of spiritual equality was a distinctive belief of the *neon ethnos* ("new race"), and by the late third and early fourth centuries, the practice of celibacy was considered the most viable means of acquiring spiritual equality.

Although celibacy was predicable of both sexes it was of particular importance sociologically for women. By adopting celibacy as an integral part of the ascetic life women became participants with men in striving toward perfection. In so doing they acquired a position of equality which mandated the creation of a new space for women other than that allotted to wife, mother, and courtesan. The rationalized confinement of women to the domestic sphere was no longer valid when a life of celibacy offered an option to marriage. Similarity of pursuits (a life of perfection by means of asceticism) tended to minimize the prevalent attitude of male/female inequality according to nature. Furthermore, women's voluntary renunciation of wealth and social class rendered them less threatening to men in

---

5. *Ibid.*, p. 166.
6. *Idem.*
7. Cf. Tertullian, *Ad Nationes* 1.8 and Apol. 42; Eusebius, *Hist. Eccl.* 1.4; and *Preaching of Peter.*

pursuit of the same religious ideals.[8]

Celibate men and women, by virtue of their "spiritual nuptials" with Christ, were considered the recipients of special intimacy with God. Like the soul-nuptials in Plato's *Symposium,* the *hieros gamos* ("sacred marriage") of the mystery religions, or the Hebrew concept of God's marriage with Israel, these Christian nuptials initiated celibates as a type of "new elite" in Christian societies.[9] The elitism was derived from the celibates' peculiar intimacy with God, an intimacy which allowed new social groupings (monastics) and a new paradigm of relationships between male and female celibates (heterosexual friendship). The previous paradigm for institutionalized relationships between men and women was that of husband/wife. Celibacy mandated a reshifting of the social structure so as to allow mutually-supportive relations outside the marriage bond. An early example was the phenomenon of *syneisaktism* ("spiritual marriage") which still adhered rather closely to the husband/wife paradigm but with the added connotation of spiritual equality. This relationship was gradually eliminated throughout most Christian areas when bishops emerged as the "head" of the extended Christian families (dioceses). Through the bishops' monopoly of political power they were able gradually to control social groupings, i.e., they became guardians of the social order. As such they expected loyalty from their increasing number of spiritual "sons and daughters."[10] Ephrem of Syria, e.g., reminded bishops that they were wedded to their congregations: "Thou hast no wife, as Abraham had Sarah: Behold, thy flock is thy wife. Bring up her children in thy faithfulness!"[11] The contemporary non-Christian would have viewed the bishop as a *patronus,* someone who undertook the protection especially of the non-married women in his congregation. Hence the male in the *syneisaktism*-relationship

---

8. That some women did not completely abandon their social status is evident from Jerome's comment (*Ep.* 108) that in Paula's convent the nuns, though dressed identically, were separated into three groups on basis of social class.

9. John Bugge, *Virginitas: An Essay in the History of a Medieval Idea* (The Hague: Martinus Nijhoff, 1975), p. 59.

10. Palladius, *Dial.* 10, PG 47:35, tells how the deaconesses at Constantinople were told to bow their heads before the new bishop as they had previously done for John Chrysostom.

11. *C. Nis.* 19.1, quoted in Robert Murray, *Symbols of Church and Kingdom: A Study in Early Syriac Tradition* (Cambridge: The University Press, 1975), p. 151.

may have been regarded as a usurper of the bishop's mandated guardianship. Consequently the bishops legislated against this practice, and by the fourth century the predominant model for the celibate life was that of the monastic, here broadly defined as an ascetic man or woman living within some communal structure.

In this chosen life-style, legitimated by references to Christ and Mary as ascetic exemplars, woman was viewed as freeing herself from the corruptibility of her natural state. By transcending nature she became spiritually equal to man pursuing the same ideals.[12] By maintaining a life of celibacy, woman was freed from the "curse" of Eve concretely exemplified in pregnancy, child-bearing, subservience to husband, etc.[13] It was in this sense that the Gospel of Thomas, for example, spoke of woman transcending her female nature and becoming male.[14]

If celibacy to some extent removed the threat of a sexually-oriented relationship, certain ascetic masters and Church Fathers prescribed that celibate women maintain a non-sexually oriented presence. Hence the proliferation of literature on celibate women's gait, facial expressions, clothing, hairstyles, etc. The rationale offered for these prescriptions was that the external had to be in harmony with one's internal aspirations and dispositions; i.e., the simplicity of external demeanor, attire, etc., symbolically portrayed the inner state of the *sponsa Christi* whose focus on the heavenly bridegroom should not allow the clutter of worldly accoutrements.[15] Hence modesty became the keynote of the prescriptions addressed to Christian celibates (and women in general) as early as the time of Paul.

Church leaders' fear of women's presence as a potential power for disorder resulted in the gradual enforcement of more restrictive measures for the women's communities. Identical garb, veils, cloister

---

12. Cf. Origen, *Comm. in Matt.* 10; Methodius, *Sympos.* 1.4 and 5; Pseudo-Clement II, *Ep. de Virg.* 15; Cyril of Jerusalem, *Catech.* 12:32; *Vita S. Syncletica,* PG 28:962; Jerome, *Ep.* 48; and *Spuria,* PG 64:40.

13. E.g., Gregory of Nyssa, *De Virg.* 3; Cyprian, *De Hab. Virg.* 22; Jerome, *Ep.* 130; etc.

14. *The Gospel of Thomas* 114. Cf. *Gospel of Philip* 71 and Palladius' comment that Olympias should be called *"anthropos,"* "a man in everything but body," *Dial.* 15, PG 47:56.

15. Cf. Basil, *De Virg.,* PG 30:705, 708, 720; Gregory of Nyssa, *Vita S. Macrinae,* PG 46:969–70 and *De Virg.,* PG 348–52; Gregory Nazianzen, *Praec. ad Virg.* PG 37:584, 598, 645; etc.

walls, etc., were used as effective anti-seductive devices to minimize or eliminate the image of woman as sensual temptress.[16] These changes to a stricter normative way of life occurred as the early Christian communities were gradually transformed into broadly extended social institutions. However, the practice of heterosexual friendship remained possible though it too became institutionalized to a certain extent.

As the monastic enclosures were more strictly enforced after the sixth century and restrictions were placed upon the earlier, less structured way of life, there was less opportunity to communicate as freely as previously. But the friendships continued through subsequent centuries of European culture. By the early Middle Ages a definite profile of women had emerged,[17] and one need only read the records of monastic establishments (particularly the double monasteries) to discern the leadership roles women acquired and maintained within their own institutions.[18]

And there were still Jeromes and Paulas, Chrysostoms and Olympias to carry on the tradition of earlier days. One reads of the consolatory, friendly correspondence and/or vocal exchange between Benedict and Scholastica, Fortunatus and Radegund, Jane de Chantal and Francis de Sales, Claire and Francis, Diana and Jordan, Catherine of Siena and Raymond of Capua, Teresa of Avila and John of the Cross. The friendship-ideal as practiced in early Christian communities was a legacy inherited by subsequent centuries. It continued to be realized in varying degrees during later periods of Christian cultures. Literary evidence demonstrating the continuation

16. Fatima Mernissi, in *Beyond the Veil: Male–Female Dynamics in a Modern Muslim Society* (Cambridge, Massachusetts: Schenkman, 1975), points out the importance of veils even in modern Islamic countries. Women must, for example, wear veils when walking in public because they are stepping outside their own territory into men's space.

17. See Frances and Joseph Gies, *Women in the Middle Ages* (New York: Thomas Y. Crowell, 1978), and Eileen Power, *Medieval Women*, ed. M. M. Postan (Cambridge: The University Press, 1975).

18. The double monasteries were usually presided over by an abbess, the most famous of which was abbess Hilda of Whitby. See Mary Bateson, "Origin and Early History of Double Monasteries," *Trans. of the Royal Historical Society*, 13 (1899), 137–98 and Giles Constable, *Medieval Monasticism* (Toronto: University of Toronto Press, 1976).

of heterosexual friendships witnesses to the permanent value of the spiritually-oriented, but humanly real, affection practiced by men and women celibates who derived consolation, exhortation, and liberation of spirit through close interpersonal relationships.